HOW TO **PASS** THE

ROYAL NAVY OFFICER ADMIRALTY INTERVIEW BOARD (AIB)

THE **TESTING** S...

expert advice on interv...

how2become

Orders: Please contact How2become Ltd,
Suite 2, 50 Churchill Square Business Centre, Kings Hill, Kent ME19 4YU.

Telephone: (44) 0845 643 1299 - Lines are open Monday to Friday 9am until 5pm.
Fax: (44) 01732 525965.
You can also order via the email address info@how2become.co.uk.

ISBN: 978-1-907558-25-2

First published 2010

Typeset for How2become Ltd. by Good Golly Design, Canada, goodgolly.ca.

Printed in Great Britain for How2become Ltd.
by Bell & Bain Ltd, 303 Burnfield Road, Thornliebank, Glasgow G46 7UQ.

CONTENTS

WELCOME

Welcome to your new guide – *How to Pass the Royal Navy Officer Selection Process*. This guide has been designed to help you prepare for, and pass the Royal Navy Officer selection process, including the Admiralty Interview Board.

The author of this guide, Richard McMunn, has spent over 20 years in both the Royal Navy and the Emergency Services. He has vast experience and knowledge in the area of Armed Forces recruitment and you will find his guidance both inspiring and highly informative. During his successful career in the Fire Service, Richard sat on many interview panels assessing candidate's to join the job. He has also been extremely successful at passing job interviews and assessments himself and has a success rate of over 90%. Follow his advice and preparation techniques carefully and you too can achieve the same levels of success in your career.

Whilst the selection process for joining the Royal Navy as an Officer is highly competitive, there are a number of things you can do in order to improve your chances of success, and they are all contained within this guide.

The guide itself has been split up into useful sections to make it easier for you to prepare for each stage. Read each section carefully and take notes as you progress. Don't ever give up on your dreams; if you really want to become an RN Officer then you *can* do it. The way to prepare for a job in the Armed Forces as an Officer is to embark on a programme of 'in depth' preparation, and this guide will show you exactly how to do just that.

If you need any further help with the Royal Navy Officer aptitude tests,

Planning Exercises, getting fit or RN Officer Interview advice, then we offer a wide range of products to assist you. These are all available through our online shop www.how2become.co.uk.

We are also now running a number of 1 Day Admiralty Interview Board preparation training courses at the following link: NavyOfficerCourse.co.uk

Once again thank you for your custom and we wish you every success in your pursuit to joining the Royal Navy as an Officer.

Work hard, stay focused and be what you want...

Best wishes,

The how2become team

The How2become Team

PREFACE

BY RICHARD MCMUNN

I spent four years of my life in the Royal Navy from the age of 17 to 21. During these four years I experienced some of the best moments of my life. The Royal Navy taught me how to be disciplined, it taught me how to be organised and it also provided me with a sound footing for a successful future. But it didn't start out all plain sailing (excuse the pun!). I initially failed the selection process for the Fleet Air Arm by failing the medical due to being overweight. I can remember sitting in the Armed Forces careers office in Preston, Lancashire at the age of 16 waiting patiently to see the Warrant Officer who would interview me as part of my application for joining the Royal Navy. I had already passed the written tests, and despite never having sat an interview before in my life, I was confident of success.

In the build up to the interview I had worked very hard studying the job that I was applying for, and also working hard on my interview technique. At the end of the interview I was told that I had easily passed and all that was left to complete was the medical. Unfortunately I was overweight at the time and I was worried that I might fail. At the medical my fears became a reality and I was told by the doctor that I would have to lose a stone in weight before they would accept me. I walked out of the doctor's surgery and began to walk to the bus stop that would take me back home three miles away. I was absolutely gutted, and embarrassed, that I had failed at the final hurdle, all because I was overweight!

I sat at the bus stop feeling sorry for myself and wondering what job I was going to apply for next. My dream of joining the Armed Forces was over and I didn't know which way to turn. Suddenly, I began to feel a sense of determination to lose the weight and get fit in the shortest time possible. It was at that particular point in my life when things would change forever. As the bus approached I remember thinking there was no time like the present for getting started on my fitness regime. I therefore opted to walk the three miles home instead of being lazy and getting the bus. When I got home I sat in my room and wrote out a 'plan of action' that would dictate how I was going to lose the weight required. That plan of action was very simple and it said the following three things:

1. Every weekday morning I will get up at 6am and run 3 miles.
2. Instead of catching the bus to college, and then back home again, I will walk.
3. I will eat healthily and I will not go over the recommended daily calorific intake.

Every day I would read my simple 'action plan' and it acted as a reminder of what I needed to do. Within a few weeks of following my plan rigidly I had lost over a stone in weight and I was a lot fitter too!

When I returned back to the doctor's surgery for my medical the doctor was amazed that I had managed to lose the weight in such a short space of time and he was pleased that I had been so determined to pass the medical. Six months later I started my basic training course with the Royal Navy.

Ever since then I have always made sure that I prepare properly for any job application. If I do fail a particular interview or section of an application process then I will always go out of my way to ask for feedback so that I can improve for next time. I also still use an 'action plan' in just about every element of my work today. Action plans allow you to focus your mind on what you want to achieve and I would strongly recommend that you use one during your preparation for the RN Officer Selection process.

Throughout my career I have always been successful. It's not because I am better than the next person, but simply because I prepare better. I didn't do very well at school so I have to work a lot harder to pass the exams and written tests that form part of a job application process, but I am always aware of what I need to do and what I must improve on.

I have always been a great believer in preparation. Preparation was my key to success, and it also yours. Without the right level of preparation you will be setting out on the route to failure. The RN is hard to join, especially as an Officer, but if you follow the steps that I have compiled within this guide and use them as part of your preparation, then you will increase your chances of success dramatically.

The men and women of the Armed Forces carry out an amazing job. They are there to protect us and our country and they do that job with great pride, passion and very high levels of professionalism and commitment. They are to be congratulated for the job that they do. Before you apply to join the RN as an Officer you need to be fully confident that you too are capable of providing that same level of commitment. If you think you can do it, and you can rise to the challenge, then you just might be the type of person the RN is looking for.

Best wishes,

Richard McMunn

Richard McMunn

WHAT'S IT LIKE IN THE ROYAL NAVY?

I can only speak from my personal experience and that of other people whom I've spoken to during the research into this guide, but the simple answer is that it's a fantastic career. It's certainly not an easy career in respect of being away from home for many weeks and even months at a time, but it is still an amazing career nonetheless. As an Officer you will have an even bigger challenge. You will be the future of the Royal Navy and you will be required to lead and motivate the men and women that you command; it is a highly responsible job.

I joined the Royal Navy as an Aircraft Engineer in the Fleet Air Arm and I served with 800 Naval Air Squadron on HMS Invincible during the early 1990's. I met lots of brilliant and talented people during my career and I formed a number of very close friendships along the way. I'd also been around the world by the time I was 19 and visited places that others only ever dream about. I can remember boarding the train at Preston station on April the 13th 1989 that would take me to HMS Raleigh for my initial training course. I'd been away from home before for a couple of weeks at the most during a school geography field trip and a scout trip, but nothing could prepare me for the basic training course that I was about to be put through. My parents and my girlfriend at the time waved me off from the platform. As the train departed I sat there with a combined feeling of adventure and apprehension. The train journey from Preston to HMS Raleigh was a long one, about 7 hours I seem to recall, just enough time for me to get even more nervous before the recruit course started. Even though it was many years ago I can still picture the Leading Hand who met me at Torpoint train station. As the train pulled in he stood there with his clipboard and stick. Just the look of him was enough to make me want to turn around and go back home! I was amazed at how many people I'd been sat on the same train with who were also on the recruit course. None of us had even realised or spoke to each other during the entire train journey. We all stood there on the platform with our bags and suitcases waiting to be told what to do by the fearsome looking Leading Hand. He carried out a roll call and once he was satisfied that everyone was in attendance we all boarded the blue Sherpa van and headed off to HMS Raleigh where we would start our basic training.

Over the next few weeks I learnt how to iron (properly), clean my shoes (properly), got very fit and learnt everything you could possibly cram into six weeks about the Royal Navy. It was an intense initiation into the service but it felt great to be a part of such an organisation. You see, when you join an organisation like this, everyone looks out for each other and you also get to forge very close friendships along the way. During my career in the Royal Navy I met loads of brilliant people. Some of the more memorable friendships were with Andy Salter, Steve Doubleday (I think he's a pilot now) Mike Tolley, Steve 'Smudge' Smith, Darryl 'Bomber' Brown, Stu Brown, Tiny O'grady and Steve Lomas, all great people with whom I shared some unbelievable times.

Once I'd completed my basic training course I then spent the next 10 moths or so at HMS Daedalus in Gosport. Here I learnt how to become an Aircraft Engineer working with weapons, ejector seats and also on the electrical systems of an aircraft. It was a steep learning curve but I loved every minute of it. Once my trade training was complete I then went off to serve with 899 Harrier Squadron which was based at Royal Naval Air Station (RNAS) Yeovilton at the time. I would basically 'cut my teeth' with 899 Squadron and learn how to service and repair Harrier jets under close supervision before finally being let loose on my own with 800 Squadron. Although based at RNAS Yeovilton, 800 Sqaudron was assigned to HMS Invincible. My first ever trip with HMS Invincible was only a few weeks long, during sea trials just off the coast of Norway. If you've ever seen an aircraft career such as the Invincible you will know that it has a 'ski ramp'. The ski ramp is basically a steep incline that the fixed wing aircraft use to take off from. If you are part of a Harrier Squadron upon an aircraft carrier then you get the unfortunate experience of sleeping directly below the ski ramp! During my time on Invincible, Harriers would take off usually six at a time during all times of the day. If you were trying to sleep directly below the ramp at the time of take off then you were usually unsuccessful, as you can imagine. Shifts on board ship for me usually consisted of 8 hours on, 8 hours off continuous without many rest days. This shift system was applicable to my squadron only and the other members of the ships company would work different hours. All I can remember is that every member of the ships company would work his or her socks off throughout the duration of the trip, even if the trip was for months at a time. It's true what they say, whilst we all sleep comfortably at night in our homes there are many thousands of British Forces men and women working tirelessly to protect us and our Country. For all the hard work however there would be the odd 'run ashore'. A run ashore is basically a trip off the boat to dry land where you can go and let your hair down, sample the local culture and have a few sociable drinks. I had some great runs ashore in places such as Barbados, Portugal, America, Italy, Africa, Spain and Greece.

Of course, you have to be on your best behaviour at all times as the last thing you want is to get into trouble whilst in another country. However, follow the rules, don't do anything stupid and you can have a great time in the process.

After serving a few years in the Navy I decided that it was time to follow my lifetime ambition of becoming a firefighter. I could have quite easily stayed in the Navy for 22 years but I had always set my heart on fighting fires. I was very young when I joined the Navy but I believe the experiences that I gained during my time set me up for a bright and successful future in the Fire Service. The Royal Navy taught me how to be disciplined, it taught me how to get organised and it also taught me how to look after myself. When I joined the Fire Service following my career in the Navy I literally breezed the selection process and I also passed the initial firefighter training course with relative ease. This was simply due to the fact that I was self disciplined and I knew how to prepare effectively, all as a result of my experiences in the Navy. One thing the Navy didn't prepare me for however was sea sickness. I spent months aboard HMS Invincible during some of the most treacherous sea conditions imaginable and I was never sea sick. However, after I passed my initial firefighter training course I was assigned to White Watch at Maidstone Fire Station. During the first few weeks on the watch I was invited to go on a sea fishing trip in a small boat just off the coast of Dover. I've never been so sea sick in all my life! How embarrassing.

The Navy is one of the few jobs where an employer, in this case the Government, is willing to take you on without any previous work experience or qualifications. Show them that you're worth the investment during the selection process, and they will develop you into a competent and professional person during your career. When I left the Navy to join the Fire Service I was a totally different man from when I first joined. At the age of 21 I had been around the world, I was physically fit, and I had a number of highly useful qualifications under my belt to boot. I will always be grateful to the Royal Navy for giving me the opportunity that they did.

So, now it's your turn. But before you join you will need to work hard in order to pass the selection process. In order to help you prepare effectively for the selection process I have split the guide up into 'easy to use' sections. Read the guide carefully and take notes as you progress. For anyone out there who believes I am not qualified to teach you how to pass the Admiralty Interview Board, think again. I have helped many people to successfully become RN

Officers through this guide and also my 1 Day Intensive RN Officer training course at NavyOfficerCourse.co.uk.

I wish you all the very best in your pursuit to joining the Royal Navy as an elite Officer,

Richard McMunn

Richard McMunn

Disclaimer

CHAPTER 1
THE SELECTION PROCESS FOR BECOMING A ROYAL NAVY OFFICER

The majority of people who will read this guide will have a thorough understanding of what the Royal Navy Officer Selection process consists of. Before I get into each element of selection however, and more importantly how to pass them, it is important for me to briefly explain the different elements.

To begin with, applicants will need to contact their local Armed Forces Careers Office and explain that they wish to apply to become an Officer with the Royal Navy. The most effective way to do this is to go along to your nearest centre for a brief chat. You will be supplied with an information pack and details on how to apply, providing you meet the minimum eligibility requirements.

THE FILTER INTERVIEW

You will eventually be invited to attend what is called a 'filter' interview. This interview is designed to assess whether or not you have the right qualities to become a Royal Navy Officer. If you successfully pass the filter interview, which is usually held at the Armed Forces Careers Office, you will be recommended to attend the Admiralty Interview Board (AIB). The filter interview is, in my opinion, relatively easy to pass. However, you will still need to put in plenty of preparation and I have provided you with a host of sample questions and responses during a later section of this guide.

THE ADMIRALTY INTERVIEW BOARD

The AIB is designed to assess whether you have the right personal qualities and attributes to become a successful Royal Navy Officer. The only way you will pass it is through hard work and determination.

There are two key elements to passing the AIB –

1) How you perform

2) How you behave

Whilst there are many different factors that can influence each element they both must be taken seriously. For example, during one of the evenings at the AIB you will be allowed to visit the bar and mix with young Officer Recruits who are part way through their training. This is not a time to get drunk and let your hair down, but a time to relax and find out as much as you can about the training you will undertake if you are to be successful at the AIB. Whilst an evening in the bar is not assessable, how you behave certainly is! The Board will naturally expect you to have found out as much as you can about the Royal Navy, and they will ask you questions about ships and equipment and your chosen specialisation so make sure you are fully prepared. It is also a good idea for you to have looked for opportunities for responsibility and personal development.

THE BIOGRAPHICAL QUESTIONNAIRE

Before you arrive at the AIB you will be sent a questionnaire to complete. This is used to inform the interviewers and to provide initial evidence; it is important that you complete this form as fully and accurately as possible. This is your chance to "blow your own trumpet" so to speak. Make sure you put yourself across in a positive manner and let them now about your achievements to date and anything else that you are currently involved in.

In order to assist you during your preparation, I have now provided you sample responses to a number of the biographical questionnaire questions.

FORM Q101
SAMPLE RESPONSES (SUCCESSFUL APPLICATION)

1. Briefly describe why you wish to become an officer in the RN, RM or RFA.

I want the challenge which the RN would give me: to achieve what I would not otherwise expect or find myself able to achieve. I've always chosen to work in teams as I flourish as a committed team member. I've been deeply impressed by the camaraderie of service personnel.

I want to make use of my past experience: a) as a leader – especially training and motivating people.

I want to contribute to and support the work of our nation's service personnel, specifically the RN as I could commit to the RN's ethos and practice.

2a. Describe a time when you have been in charge of a project or have had to lead a team, and what you did.

When my manager left the company in 2005 I was initially given his role temporarily. It was my task to maintain all services within the company until a new manager was appointed. My priorities were: delegation, communication and motivation. I set up and led a monthly meeting of all the supervisors together from company, as well as a weekly contact with each employee within my team. I appointed one of the supervisors to act as the point of contact for all members of staff in case they needed support during the interim period. I asked each of the other supervisors to take responsibility for organising elements of their own team and stated that I would be the point of contact for them if they needed advice, guidance or assistance. Once this new administrative system was in place, my priority was to motivate the supervisors and staff, especially during setbacks.

2b. Describe a time when you have been part of a team, including details of your own role within that team.

In 2008 I was one of four crew on-board a 48 foot yacht, sailing from the Azores to Plymouth. None of us had previously sailed offshore for such a distance, nor had we previously met each other. The skipper divided us into two groups so that we could 'hot bunk' the berths and we worked watches day and night. The four crews shared on a rota basis the responsibilities of: navigation, sail trimming, keeping watch, helming, weather forecasting, washing up, cleaning cabins, the galley and the heads. The weather varied from relatively no wind to Force 9, gusting Force 10, during which I was the only crew who volunteered to helm. I'd recently passed the RYA Ocean Yacht master course (theory) so was able to practice some astronavigation.

3. Describe a time when you have set yourself a challenging goal or target and endeavoured to achieve it, including information on the outcome.

In 2006 I decided that I wanted to raise money for a local charity. The aim was to raise £10,000 in total. In order to achieve this, I set myself the challenge of completing an iron-man challenge which included swimming 2 kilometres, running a marathon before finally cycling 120 miles, all in one day. I started out by planning my training routine and decided that I would need 6 months to complete the task. I gradually increased my distances over time and ensured that I ate healthily and avoided alcohol and junk food in the build up to my challenge. I used an action plan that determined when I would train. Whilst training, I also took control of fundraising, writing to large local companies requesting sponsorship. The end result was that I completed the challenge in 9 hours and 43 minutes, raising £10.784 in the process for a local children's charity.

Let's now take a look at the AIB and what each day consists of.

DAY ONE AIB

On arrival at HMS Sultan you will be directed to the AIB complex where you will be introduced and provided with a briefing about the next 3 days selection.

Once the brief is completed you will then be split up into groups of 3 or 4 depending on the size of the overall group. All of the tests that you will undertake over the 3 days are completed in these groups so that you get to know your team. This will also provide the AIB staff with an idea of how you will perform with other men and women. It is important that you are comfortable with working with people of the opposite sex and also people from different backgrounds and cultures. The first night at the AIB is usually your own free time.

DAY TWO AIB

The first morning will see you get up at approx 6.15am. You will be required to sit your first tests in the examining room at 7.30am so you can see why it is best to get an early night the evening before. During the first batch of tests you will sit a number of psychometric tests; general naval knowledge tests and you will also be required to write an essay.

Examples of Royal Navy General Knowledge Questions

I have now provided you with examples of both Royal Navy and Royal Marines general knowledge questions. As part of your preparation, go away and find out the answer to each of the questions.

NOTE: Although you are applying to become a Royal Navy Officer it is still advisable that you take the time to learn about the Royal Marines too. After all, they form part of the Royal Navy.

1. What aircraft does the Royal Navy currently use?
2. What is the rank badge of Warrant Officer?
3. Which ships carry aircraft & what types do they carry?
4. Which insignia denotes a Lieutenant Commander?
5. What does N.A.T.O stand for?
6. How much is the annual Royal Navy Budget?
7. What type of missile is the Sea Dart?
8. What is the range of the Side Winder missile?
9. What is the rank badge of a Chief Petty Officer?
10. What is the beam of a ship?
11. How many countries are in NATO?
12. Name the UK naval bases?
13. What is the name of the military operations in Afghanistan?

14. What is the role of a survey ship?
15. What is the displacement of an aircraft carrier?
16. How many are a typical frigate crew?
17. Give examples of typical weapons of a submarine?
18. How many naval personnel are there approximately?
19. What does CIWS stand for?
20. What weapons do the Type 45 destroyers carry?
21. How long is the initial commission as an officer?
22. What was the name of Nelson's ship at the battle of Trafalgar?
23. What is the displacement of the New Type 45 Destroyer?
27. What is the main weapon system fitted to the new Astute submarines?
24. What type of engines are fitted to the Type 22 and Type 23 Frigates?
25. HMS Endurance is what kind of Ship?

Examples of RM Knowledge Questions

1. What types of helicopter do the Royal Marines use?
2. Name a Landing platform helicopter and a Landing platform dock?
3. What is the rank slide of a regimental sergeant major?
4. Where are the three commando units based?
5. How many men can be carried in a LCVP?
6. How many men are there in a commando unit?
7. How many men are there in the Royal Marines?
8. Which ATV does the Royal Marines use?
9. What is the name of the new commando structure?
10. At what rank do you enter the Royal Mrines as an officer?
11. How many men are there in a platoon?
12. What is the corps motto?
13. What is the highest rank in the Royal Marines?
14. In what year was the battle of Trafalgar?
15. What weapon does a Royal Marines rifleman carry?

16. Which anti tank weapons does the Royal Marines employ?
17. What happens to injured recruits during training?
18. What time is allowed for a Royal Marines officer to complete the 30 mile speed march?
19. What happened at Walcheren?
20. List 10 Royal Marines specialisations?
21. What are the Commando Tests?
22. How long is the Royal Marines recruit training?
23. What is the Corps birth date?
24. When were the Commandos founded?

Once you have worked out the answer to each of the above questions, take the time to complete the following General Knowledge test.

NOTE: RN = Royal Navy; RM = Royal Marines

GENERAL SERVICE KNOWLEDGE TEST

Question 1

RN - How many weeks is the initial Royal Navy Officer training course.

RM - How many months is the Young Officer training course?

Answers

Question 2

RN - Where does initial Royal Navy Officer training take place at?

RM - Where does initial Royal Marines Officer training take place at?

Answers

Question 3

RN - During term 1 of Royal Navy Officer training you will learn 5 'Key Pillars'. What are these?

RM - During Month 3 of Royal Marines Officer YO training, what gun will you be introduced to?

Answers

Question 4

RN - What is the highest rank for Ratings?

RM – What is the highest Commando rank?

Answers

Question 5

RN - Where is the Royal Navy Command Headquarters based at?

Answers

Question 6

RN - Who has full command of the Royal Navy Fleet and is responsible for Fleet element of military operational capability?

RM – Who is the current Commandant General Royal Marines?

Answers

Question 7

RN - What is the name of the flag that is worn by all HM Ships in commission and by shore establishments?

RM – What is the Royal Marines motto?

Answers

Question 8

What is the name given to the procedure where a Royal Navy ship is re-supplied with fuel, food, stores and ammunition whilst at sea?

Answers

Question 9

RN - What is the highest Officer rank in the Royal Navy?

RM – What is the highest Officer rank in the Royal Marines?

Answers

Question 10

RN - At cruising speed, what is the maximum distance a Royal Navy frigate can travel?

RM – What are the 10 Royal Marines command values?

Answers

Question 11

RN - At cruising speed, what is the maximum distance a Royal Navy destroyer can travel?

RM – Where are the following Commando Units based: 40, 42 and 45?

Answers

Question 12

RN - Which of the following is not a Type 23 Duke Class Frigate?

HMS Argyll
HMS Lancaster
HMS Gloucester
HMS Iron Duke

RM - 3 Commando Brigade is on permanent operational readiness and is a core component of what?

Answers

Question 13

RN - Which of the following is not a Type 42 Destroyer?

HMS Liverpool
HMS Edinburgh
HMS York
HMS Daring

RM – What is the definition of 'ethos'?

Answers

Question 14

RN - Which of the following is/was not a Naval Air Squadron?

NAS 800
NAS 727
NAS 820
NAS 814
NAS 722

RM – Which Commando Unit is based at Norton Manor Camp?

Answers

Question 15

RN - In 2002 which of the following Royal Navy training establishments became the lead establishment for the Maritime Warfare School (MWS)?

HMS Excellent
HMS Collingwood
HMS Sultan
HMS Dartmouth

RM – Which Commando Unit was formed in August 1943?

Answers [ ]

ANSWERS TO GENERAL ROYAL NAVY QUIZ

1. 28 weeks for RN Officer and 15.5 months for RM Officer.
2. BRNC Dartmouth / Lympstone.
3. Maritime, Military, Staff, Command Leadership and Management, Grit/ Courage. GPMG.
4. Warrant Officer 1 for both RN and RM
5. Portsmouth
6. Commander in Chief Fleet / Major General F H R Howes
7. White Ensign / 'Per Mare Per Terram', 'By Sea By Land'
8. Replenishment at Sea or RAS
9. Admiral of the Fleet / Major General
10. 7,500 miles / Courage, cheerfulness, unity, professional, standards, determination, fortitude, adaptability, commando humour, unselfishness.
11. 4,000 miles / Taunton (40 Commando), Plymouth (42 Commando) and Arbroath (45 Commando).
12. HMS Gloucester / The UK's Joint Rapid Reaction Force.
13. HMS Daring / "What a group does and how it does it"
14. NAS 722 / 40
15. HMS Collingwood / 42

THE QUALITES REQUIRED TO BECOME A ROYAL NAVY OFFICER

Many candidates who attend Admiralty Interview Board will be under prepared. In addition to this, many candidates will spend hours scouring internet chat forums in an attempt to find hints and tips on how to pass AIB. Whilst there is nothing wrong with this, the most effectively prepared candidates are those who concentrate primarily on demonstrating the key assessable qualities in order to become a Royal Navy Officer.

The whole purpose of the AIB is to determine whether or not you have the 'potential' to become a Naval Officer. If you have the potential then there is a greater chance that you will pass Initial Training Course. The Royal Navy will be investing literally hundreds of thousands of pounds into your development and career progression. Therefore, they want to be sure that you have the potential to pass every stage of training.

In order to assess the potential, the Royal Navy will assess you against a series of qualities and competencies. Before I move on to the scoring criteria I want to talk a little about the qualities that you need to demonstrate during the entire selection process. You will notice that after each list of qualities I have provided you with some useful tips.

Qualities that you need to demonstrate

- Determined
- Resolute
- Persistent
- Unwavering
- Steady
- Able to overcome most difficulties
- Strong-willed.

TIPS: You are applying to join the Royal Navy as an Officer. Therefore, it is crucial that you are able to remain calm in a crisis, be totally focused on achieving the end result and be determined to succeed at everything you do.

For example, during the planning exercise stage you will be placed under considerable pressure by the assessing Officer's. If you do not know the answer to a question then it is better to say so, rather than panic, waffle or crumble under the pressure. One of the main purposes of Admiralty Interview Board is to determine whether or not you have the ability to stay focused under pressure.

- Imaginative
- Initiative
- Constructive
- Perceptive
- Original
- Mentally agile
- Inventive
- Visionary
- Intelligent
- Mature
- Balanced.

TIPS: These qualities are predominantly focused on your state of mind. Do you have the ability to come up with solutions to problems? Can you think outside the box? Can you see the end result? Are you sensible and mature for your years? During every stage of the AIB make sure you remain level-headed. Do not act in a foolhardy way and always think before you speak. Engage your brain before you engage your mouth!

- Forceful
- Compelling
- Persuasive
- Powerful
- Vigorous
- Assertive
- Consistent
- Effective
- Resourceful
- Magnetic

- Inspiring
- Considerate
- Considerable impact.

TIPS: Let us assume that you are participating in the Planning Exercise phase. You have worked hard during your preparation in the build up to AIB and you are very confident that your plan of tackling the exercise is the most effective. However, two other members of your group have alternative solutions to the problem. What do you do? The options are simple – you can either go along with their desired solutions(s) or you can have the confidence in your own abilities and your plan and attempt to 'persuade' them both that your option is the most effective. If I was attending AIB, I would have the confidence in my own abilities and persuade them that my option is the most effective.

Remember – you are applying to become a Royal Navy Officer and that means you are applying to become a leader!

- Bold
- Daring
- Courageous
- Entrepreneurial
- Enthusiastic
- Spirit of adventure
- Untiring
- Energetic
- Active
- Diligent
- Industrious
- Persevering
- Physically strong and active
- Organiser
- Sense of urgency.

TIPS: During Practical Leadership Task (PLT), be sure to get involved. Those people, who believe that if they sit on the fence and don't get involved will go unnoticed, are sorely mistaken. You must get involved, come up with solutions, encourage the team, support others and try your hardest to achieve every task that you are set. When it is your turn to take command, do so. Do not be weak; be strong, confident and in control at all times. More on this later.

- Tolerant
- Flexible
- Co-operative
- Diplomatic
- Tactful
- Resilient (never gives in)
- Adaptable
- Willing to accept responsibility.

TIPS: What are you like towards other people? Do you have the ability to work with others as part of a team? Every team encounters problems along the way. How you deal with those problems is what matters. Be tolerant of other people, always be flexible in your approach to tasks, never give in and be the first to put your hand up when they ask for a volunteer.

- Sensible
- Respective
- Shrewd
- Well-balanced
- Decisive
- Discerning
- Fair
- Unbiased
- Loyal
- Steadfast.

I have now provided you with plenty of qualities that all go towards making an effective Royal Navy Officer. So, when the interview panel asks you the question "What are the qualities of a Royal Navy Officer?" you will have no problem answering it!

YOU ARE A LEADER AND A MANAGER

Royal Navy Officers are both leaders and managers. Therefore, it is important that you understand the difference between each of them and how they are interlinked.

In order to become a competent Naval Officer you will need to be effective at both. Here's a brief explanation of how they differ:

Leader – A leader is someone who effectively takes a team of people from point A to point B. These two 'points' don't have to be in terms of distance, but instead they could be a mission or a company or organisational goal. For example, it might be a football manager attempting to lead his or her team to promotion to a higher league. A leader should be a visionary. They should 'see' where they want their team to be and take steps to get them there.

Manager – A manager is someone who arranges and uses resources in order to achieve a companies or organisations goal. Examples of resources are:

- People
- Utilities such as water, gas and electricity
- Vehicles and equipment
- Paper and pencils
- Fuel
- Time

An effective manager will use his or her resources effectively. They will not waste resources and they will use them appropriately. A manager's greatest asset is his/her people whom which they command. When you join the Royal Navy as an Officer you will undoubtedly be responsible at some point in your career for a group or team of people. How you manage them is very important.

HOW DO THEY WORK TOGETHER?

During my time in the Fire Service I served as an Officer for many years. Without wishing to blow my own trumpet, I was a highly effective manager and leader. Managerial and leadership skills are interlinked and you will draw on each of these assets at different times during your career as a Royal Navy Officer. For example, whilst attending severe fires and road traffic collisions in the Fire Service, I was required to use both leadership and managerial skills at the same time in order to achieve the required task. I would always have a plan that was discussed with my Junior Officers. I would assign people and equipment (resources) to carry out certain tasks at the incident. I would order equipment, fuel and refreshments (resources) well in advance of them running out. I would arrange many hours in advance for relief crews to attend the incident in order to replace my tiring firefighters. I would support my team and I would communicate effectively with them during every stage of the incident. At the end of the incident I would always hold an incident debrief. This would allow me to thank everyone for their efforts and allow us to identify any areas of improvement for future incidents.

All of these actions were using my 'managerial' skills. In terms of leadership skills, I would brief my team well in order to explain the plan and what it was that needed to be done. I would provide words of support and encouragement throughout the operation and I would listen carefully to my junior officer's advice and suggestions during every stage of the incident.

Being an officer in the Navy is about drawing on different skills and assets in order to achieve a task or goal. That goal may take many years to achieve and may not necessarily be a short term objective. Always remember that in order to become a competent Royal Navy Officer, you will need to be an effective leader and manager.

CHAPTER 2
THE ROYAL NAVY OFFICER FILTER INTERVIEW

THE ROYAL NAVY OFFICER FILTER INTERVIEW AND HOW TO PASS IT

During the Royal Navy Officer selection process you will be required to sit interviews at both the Armed Forces Careers Office (AFCO) and during your attendance at the Admiralty Interview Board (AIB). Whilst the questions and tips contained within this section of the guide concentrate primarily on the AFCO interview, they are also great preparation for the AIB too. The interview, which is held at your local Armed Forces Careers Office, will be undertaken by a member of the Royal Navy recruitment team. The purpose of this interview is to 'filter' out those people who have the potential to become an RN Officer. If you have the potential, then you will get put forward to attend the AIB.

The duration of the initial AFCO interview will very much depend on your responses to the questions. However, you can expect the interview to last for approximately 30 minutes. The questions that you will be assessed against during the initial interview will normally be taken from the following areas:

> The reasons why you want to join the Royal Navy and why you have chosen this service over the Army and the Royal Air Force;

> Why you want to become a Royal Navy officer and what skills, qualities and experiences you have that would help you to become a competent Officer.

> What choice of career you are most interested in, the reason for choosing that career, and the skills you have to match the role;

> What information you already know about the Royal Navy, its history, its lifestyle and training;

> Information relating to your hobbies and interests including sporting/ team activities;

> Any personal responsibilities that you currently have at home, in your education or at work;

> Information about your family and your partner and what they think about you joining.

> Information based around your initial application;

> Your experience of work and education;

> Your emotional stability and your maturity;

> Your drive and determination to succeed.

> Having a positive reaction to a disciplined environment and towards people in positions of authority.

Before I move on to a number of sample interview questions and responses I want to explain a little bit about interview technique and how you can come across in a positive manner during the interview. During my career in the Fire Service I sat on many interview panels assessing people who wanted to become firefighters. As you can imagine there were some good applicants and there were also some poor ones. Let me explain the difference between a good applicant and a poor one.

A GOOD APPLICANT

A good applicant is someone who has taken the time to prepare. They have researched both the organisation they are applying to join and also the role that they are being interviewed for. They may not know every detail about the organisation and the role but it will be clear that they have made an effort to find out important facts and information. They will be well presented at the interview and they will be confident, but not over confident. As soon as they walk into the interview room they will be polite and courteous and they will sit down in the interview chair only when invited to do so. Throughout the interview they will sit up right in the chair and communicate in a positive manner. If they do not know the answer to a question they will say so and they won't try and waffle. At the end of the interview they will ask positive questions about the job or the organisation before shaking hands and leaving.

A POOR APPLICANT

A poor applicant could be any combination of the following. They will be late for the interview or even forget to turn up at all. They will have made little effort to dress smart and they will have carried out little or no preparation. When asked questions about the job or the organisation they will have little or no knowledge. Throughout the interview they will appear to be unenthusiastic about the whole process and will look as if they want the interview to be over as soon as possible. Whilst sat in the interview chair they will slouch and fidget. At the end of the interview they will try to ask clever questions that are intended to impress the panel.

I strongly advise that you try out a mock interview before the real thing. You'll be amazed at how much your confidence will improve. All you need to do is get your parents or a friend to sit down with you and ask you the interview questions that are contained within this guide. Try the answer them as if you were at the real interview. The more mock interviews you try the more confident you'll become.

INTERVIEW TECHNIQUE

How you present yourself during the interview is important. Whilst assessing candidates for interviews I will not only assess their responses to the interview questions but I will also pay attention to the way they present themselves. A candidate could give excellent responses to the interview questions but if they present themselves in a negative manner then this can lose them marks.

Take a look at the following diagrams which indicate both poor technique and good technique.

POOR INTERVIEW TECHNIQUE

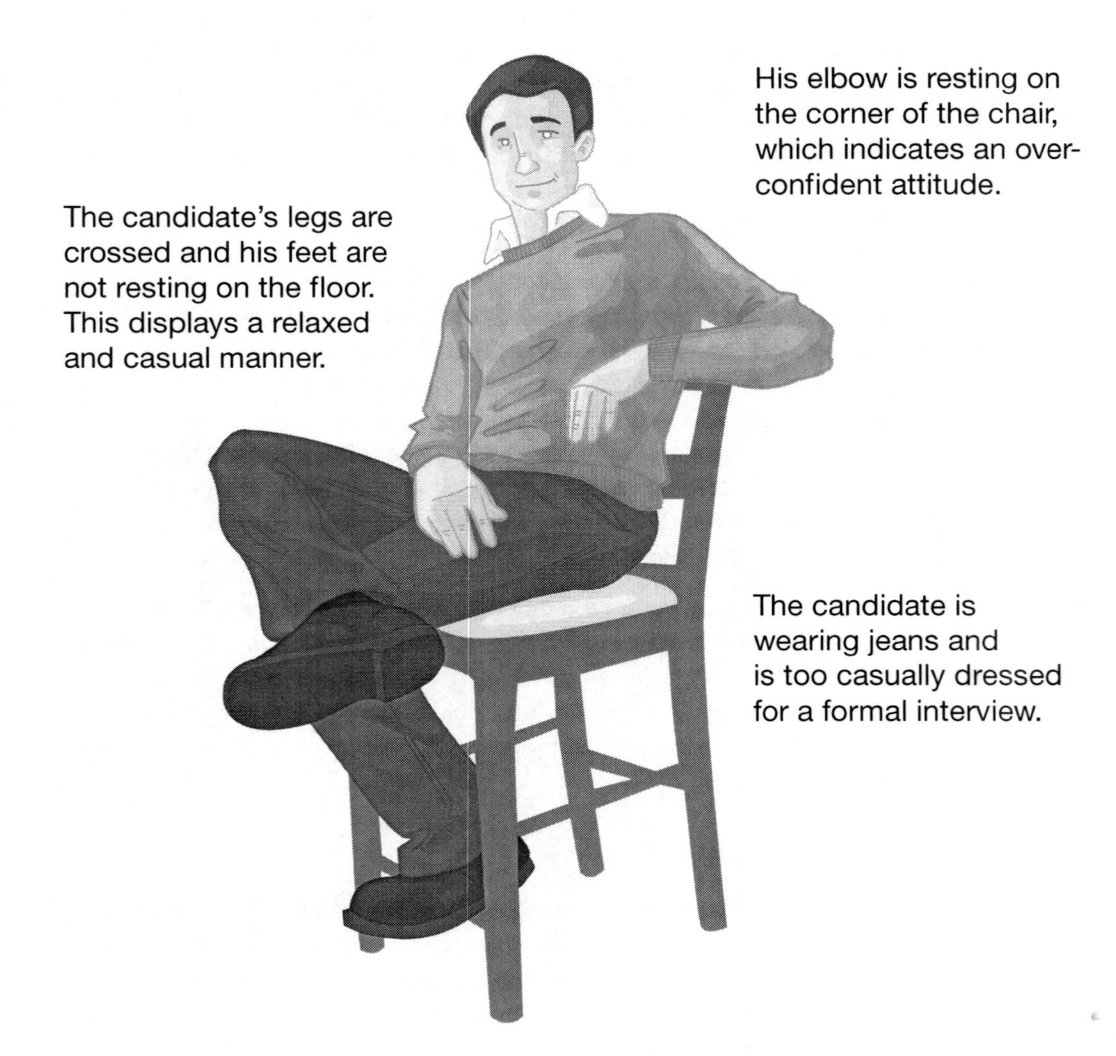

The candidate appears to be too relaxed and casual for an interview.

GOOD INTERVIEW TECHNIQUE

The candidate is smiling and he portrays a confident, but not over-confident manner.

The candidate is dressed wearing a smart suit. It is clear that he has made an effort in his presentation.

His hands are in a stable position, which will prevent him from fidgeting. He could also place his hands palms facing downwards and resting on his knees.

He is sitting upright in the interview chair with his feet resting on the floor. He is not slouching and he portrays himself in a positive manner.

In the build up to your initial AFCO interview practice a few 'mock' interviews. Look to improve your interview technique as well as working on your responses to the interview questions.

Now let's take a look at a number of sample interview questions. Please note that these questions are not guaranteed to be the exact ones you'll come up against at the real interview, but they are great starting point in your preparation. Use the sample responses that I have provided as a basis for your own preparation. Construct your answers on your own opinions and experiences.

SAMPLE INTERVIEW QUESTION NUMBER 1

Why do you want to join the Royal Navy?

This is an almost guaranteed question during the Officer Filter interview so there should be no reason why you can't answer it in a positive manner. Only you will know the real reason why you want to join but consider the following benefits before you construct your response:

> A career in the Royal Navy is challenging. You will face challenges that are not usually available in normal jobs outside of the Armed Forces. These challenges will make you a better person and they will develop you into a professional and competent member of a proud organisation;

> A career in the Royal Navy will not only give you the chance to develop your skills and potential but it will also give you excellent qualifications and training;

> A career in the Royal Navy will give you the chance to travel and see different cultures. This alone will broaden your horizons and make you a more rounded person;

> The Royal Navy, like the other Armed Forces, is an organisation that people have a huge amount of respect for. Therefore those people who join it are very proud to be a part of such a team.

Try to display a good level of motivation when answering questions of this nature. The Royal Navy is looking for people who want to become a professional member of their team and who understand their way of life. It should be your own decision to join and you should be attracted to what this career has to offer. If you have been pushed into joining by your family then you shouldn't be there. There now follows a sample response to this question.

SAMPLE RESPONSE TO INTERVIEW QUESTION NUMBER 1

Why do you want to join the Royal Navy?

'I have been working towards my goal of joining the Royal Navy as an Officer for a number of years now. A couple of years ago a careers advisor visited our school to talk about the Royal Navy. After his presentation I went up to him and asked a few questions about the different career options that were available. In particular I was most interested in the role of an Officer as I believe I have the leadership and management potential to succeed in this role. Since that day I have set my sights on joining this organisation and I have been working hard to improve myself. To be honest, I want a career that will give me direction, professional training, qualifications and the chance to work with people who set themselves very high standards. I have spoken to a friend who already works in the Royal Navy as a pilot and he fully recommends it.

I've looked at the different career options outside of the Royal Navy and nothing matches up to the challenge or the sense of pride I would feel by joining a team like this. I am the Captain of the school Rugby squad and being part of a winning team is something that I very much enjoy. Even though I am quite capable of working on my own I much prefer to work in a team where everyone is working towards the same goal. Finally, even though I have a good stable home life I can't wait to leave home and see what's out there. Even though travelling isn't the be all and end all, I am looking forward to visiting different countries and experiencing varied cultures. Many of my friends have never been out of their home town but that's not for me. I want to broaden my skills and get some decent training in the process and I believe that I would be a great asset to the Royal Navy.'

SAMPLE INTERVIEW QUESTION NUMBER 2

Why have you chosen the Royal Navy over the Army or the Royal Air Force?

As you know, there are three main forces that you can apply to join. The Royal Navy is different to the other forces in the way that you'll be required to serve on board ship for many months of your career. To some, this is not appealing. Personally I enjoyed my time on board ship. I spent my time in the Fleet Air Arm which meant that I didn't spend half as much time on board ship as the other branches of the Royal Navy. Other branches will live on board ship 365 days a year, even when it is dockside. You need to be fully comfortable with this fact and be 100% certain that you can cope with the demands of living on board. Personally I believe there is nothing better than being on board ship and when you do arrive back home after a long trip it makes you appreciate your home soil even more.

The Royal Navy will give you so much variety and it will also give you many different career options. As an Officer you will receive the highest standard of training available. The Officers whom which I served with were excellent leaders, motivators and a real inspiration to the team. The amount of activity, skills and experience that I crammed into my Royal Navy career was unbelievable. You won't get that in any other job!

Take a look at the following sample response to this question before creating your own based on your own views and opinions.

SAMPLE RESPONSE TO INTERVIEW QUESTION NUMBER 2

Why have you chosen the Royal Navy over the Army or the Royal Air Force?

'I did consider the other forces and even had a chat with each of the careers advisors but at the end I was still set on the Royal Navy. I even sat down with my parents and we wrote down the benefits of each of the different services and the Royal Navy came out on top in all aspects. I have always had a keen passion to work on aircraft and it is my intention to become an Aircraft Engineering Officer. The Fleet Air Arm is my first choice because I would get to work on board ship in addition to working on aircraft. During my research I visited the Fleet Air Arm museum at HMS Heron and I was fascinated at the history and the aircraft that have formed part of the service over the years.

I have thought long and hard about my choice of career and I am fully aware of the training that I will undergo if I am successful. I've been working hard to pass the selection process and the Admiralty Interview Board and I am 100% certain that the Royal Navy is for me. If I am unsuccessful at this attempt then I will look at what I need to improve on and work hard for next time.'

SAMPLE INTERVIEW QUESTION NUMBER 3

What does your family think of you wanting to join the Royal Navy?

What your family think about you wanting to join the Royal Navy is very important, simply for the reason that you will need their support both during your training and during your career. I can remember my parents being fully behind my decision to join the Royal Navy and I'm glad that they were for a very good reason. After about two weeks into my basic training I started to feel a little bit home sick; like any young man would do being away from home for a long period of time. I rang my father and discussed with him how I felt. After about five minutes chat on the phone I felt perfectly fine and I no longer felt homesick. During that conversation he reminded me how hard I had worked to get a place on the course and that he and my mother wanted me to succeed. For that reason alone I was glad that I had the support of my parents.

Before you apply to join the Royal Navy it is important that you discuss your choice of career with either your parents or your guardian. If you have a partner then obviously you will need to discuss this with them too. If they have any concerns whatsoever then I would advise you take them along with you to the Armed Forces Careers Office so they can discuss these concerns with the trained recruitment staff. Get their full support as you may need it at some point during your career, just like I did.

There now follows a sample response to help you prepare.

SAMPLE RESPONSE TO INTERVIEW QUESTION NUMBER 3

What does your family think of you wanting to join the Royal Navy?

'Before I made my application I discussed my choice of career with both my parents and my girlfriend. Initially they were apprehensive but they could see how motivated and excited I was as I explained everything I had learnt so far about the service. I showed them the recruitment literature and we even planned a trip to the Fleet Air Arm museum so they could see what I would be joining. I understand that it is important they support me during my application as an Officer and I now have their full backing. In fact, they are now more excited about the fact I'll be leaving home than I am! I have also told them everything I know about the training I will go through and the conditions I will serve under. They are aware that the Royal Navy has a brilliant reputation and this has helped them to further understand why I want to join.

SAMPLE INTERVIEW QUESTION NUMBER 4

What grades did you achieve at school and how do you feel about them?

Questions that relate to your education are common during the Officer selection interview. In addition to this question they may also ask you questions that relate to which schools or educational establishments you attended.

This kind of question is designed to assess your attitude to your grades and also how hard you worked whilst at school, college or university. As you can imagine, your grades will generally reflect how hard you worked and therefore you will need to be totally honest in your response. Naturally you must meet the minimum eligibility requirements for becoming an Officer in the Royal Navy before you can apply, but how well you did at school or university academically, might be a reflection as to how well you will do during initial and on-going officer training. If your results were not as good as you anticipated then you will need to provide a good reason for this. If you achieved the grades you wanted during education then congratulations, you'll find this question easier to answer.

Take a look at the following sample response which is tailored towards a person who did not do as well as they wished.

SAMPLE RESPONSE INTERVIEW QUESTION NUMBER 4

What grades did you achieve at school and how do you feel about them?

'To be totally honest I didn't do as well as I had hoped. The reason for this was that I didn't work hard enough during the build up to the exams. I did put in some preparation but I now realise I should have worked harder. Whilst I passed the exams I know that I could have done a lot better. I fully appreciate that I will have several exams and assessments to pass during initial officer training and I have been preparing for this. I have embarked on an evening class at my local college to maintain my competence in Maths and English and I am constantly studying Naval facts and history. My current affairs knowledge is excellent and I have been enjoying the study time immensely. I can assure you that, even though I should have done better at university, I have learnt from this and I am working very hard to prepare for officer training in the anticipation that I am successful at AIB.'

SAMPLE INTERVIEW QUESTION NUMBER 5

What responsibilities do you have either at work, school or at home?

When you join the Royal Navy as an officer you will need to take full responsibility for yourself, your team, your equipment and also for the safety of your work colleagues. At the age of 18 I was responsible for servicing and maintaining Sea Harrier jets on board HMS Invincible. I was responsible for going out on deck at 4am in the morning and servicing the ejector seats that formed part of the pilot's safety equipment. That was a huge amount of responsibility to undertake. Whatever branch you decide to join you will need to demonstrate during selection that you can handle responsibility. The most effective way to do this is by providing the interviewer with examples of where you have already held positions of responsibility either at home, work or during your education.

Take a look at the following sample response to this question.

SAMPLE RESPONSE TO INTERVIEW QUESTION NUMBER 5

What responsibilities do you have either at work, school or at home?

'I currently hold a large number of responsibilities both at home and in my part time job. I am responsible for cleaning the house top to bottom once a week and I usually do this on a Sunday before I go and play football for my local team. I'm also captain of the football team which means I have to arrange the fixtures, book the football ground and I also collect the kit at the end of the match and get it washed and dried for the following week's fixture. I also take control of the clubs financial affairs as I have an interest in accountancy. I thoroughly enjoy this responsibility and would not have it any other way; I am always the first to volunteer for any task or role that involves a level of responsibility. In addition to this I have just started a new part-time job at my local supermarket as a junior supervisor. This involves managing five members of staff, managing stock levels and also managing resources. It is essential that I make sure the store has sufficient resources to operate effectively everyday that it is open.

I enjoy taking on responsibility as it gives me a sense of achievement. I understand that I will need to be responsible during my Royal Navy Officer

training not only for myself, but also for ensuring that I work hard to pass every assessment in order to develop into a competent Naval Officer.'

SAMPLE INTERVIEW QUESTION NUMBER 6

How do you think you will cope with the discipline, regimentation and routine in the Royal Navy?

When you join the Royal Navy you will be joining a military organisation that has set procedures, standards and discipline codes. Procedures, standards and discipline codes are there for a very good reason. They ensure that the organisation operates at its optimum best and without them things would go wrong, and people would either be injured or at worst killed. As an officer you will have the added responsibility of ensuring those underneath your command respect these important codes of conduct and policies. To some people these important aspects of service life will come as a shock when they join. The recruitment staff will want to know that you are fully prepared for this change in lifestyle. They are investing time, effort and resources into your training so they want to know that you can cope with their way of life.

When answering this type of question you need to demonstrate both your awareness of what Royal Navy life involves and also your positive attitude towards the disciplined environment. Study the recruitment literature and visit the careers website to get a feel for the type of training you will be going through.

SAMPLE RESPONSE TO INTERVIEW QUESTION NUMBER 6

How do you think you will cope with the discipline, regimentation and routine in the Royal Navy?

'I believe I would cope with it very well. In the build up to selection I have been trying to implement routine and discipline into my daily life. I've been getting up at 6am every weekday morning and going on a 3 mile run. This will hopefully prepare me for the early starts that I'll encounter during training. I've also been learning how to iron my own clothes and I've been helping around the house with the cleaning and washing. I already have to follow and manage codes of conduct in my part-time job. Being responsible for five members of staff I am required to monitor their performance, brief them on new policies and procedures, and also carry out annual appraisals.

I fully understand that the Royal Navy needs a disciplined workforce if it is to function as effectively as it does. Without that discipline things could go wrong and if I did not carry out my duties professionally then I could endanger somebody's life. I am also aware that I will be required to manage discipline within my team once I am a qualified officer. I am fully prepared for this and would carry out my duties diligently, professionally and competently.'

SAMPLE INTERVIEW QUESTION NUMBER 7

How do you think you will cope with being away from home and losing your personal freedom?

This type of question is one that needs to be answered positively. The most effective way to respond to it is to provide the recruitment staff with examples of where you have already lived away from home for a period of time. This could be either with your school or college, an adventure trip, camping with friends or even with a youth organisation. Try to think of occasions when you have had to fend for yourself or even 'rough it' during camps or adventure trips. If you are already an active person who spends very little time sat at home in front of the television or computer, then you will probably have no problem with losing your personal freedom. During your time in the Navy there'll be very little time to sit around doing nothing anyway. So, if you're used to being active before you join, then this is a plus.

Take a look at the sample response on the following page and try to structure your own response around this.

SAMPLE RESPONSE TO INTERVIEW QUESTION NUMBER 7

How do you think you will cope with being away from home and losing your personal freedom?

'I already have some experience of being away from home so I know that this would not be a problem for me. Whilst serving with the Sea Cadets I was introduced to the Navy way of life and I fully understand what it is like to be away from home. Having said that, I am not complacent and I have been working hard to improve my fitness and academic skills. To be honest with you, I'm not the kind of person who sits around at home watching television or sitting at the computer, so I'm hardly in doors anyway. In terms of losing my personal freedom I'm looking forward to the routine and regimentation that the Navy will provide as I believe this will bring some positive structure to my

life. Even though I am young I want to ensure that I have a good future and I believe a career in the Royal Navy will bring me just that, providing that is, I work hard during training.

During my time in the Sea Cadets I've been away on a couple of camps and I really enjoyed this. We learnt how to fend for ourselves whilst away and I loved the fact that I was meeting new and interesting people. I understand that the training will be difficult and intense but I am fully prepared for this. I am confident that I will cope with the change in lifestyle very well.'

SAMPLE INTERVIEW QUESTION NUMBER 8

Are you involved in any sporting activities and how do you keep yourself fit?

During the selection interview you will be asked questions that relate to your sporting activities and also how you keep yourself fit.

If you are the type of person who spends too much time on the computer or social networking sites then now's the time to make a positive change. Even though you'll be on board ship there will still be time for sporting activities. Whilst on board HMS Invincible I really got into my weight training. Right at the bottom of the ship there was a small gym, and even though it was usually packed full of Royal Marines, there was still time to keep fit. On the odd occasion when the flight deck wasn't being used for flying operations it was opened up for running and general sports such as volleyball. All of these helped to keep up the team morale on board ship.

SAMPLE RESPONSE TO INTERVIEW QUESTION NUMBER 8

Are you involved in any sporting activities and how do you keep yourself fit?

'I am an extremely fit and active person and I am currently involved in a couple of sports teams. To begin with, I visit the gym four times a week and carry out a light weight session before swimming half a mile in the pool. Sometimes I like to vary the gym session with a workout on the indoor rowing machine. In the build up to selection I have been getting up at 6am every weekday morning and going on a 3 mile run. This I believe will prepare me for the early starts during selection.

I am also a member of my local hockey team and I practice with them one evening a week during the season. We usually play one patch a week which forms part of a Sunday league table. We are currently third in the table and are pushing hard for the top spot. Finally I am a keen hill walker and love to take off for long walks in the Lake District or Brecon Beacons with some of my friends. We usually camp out for a couple of nights over a weekend so I am used to fending for myself. I am not the type of person who just sits at home on the computer or playing video games. I love being active and always keep myself fit.'

SAMPLE INTERVIEW QUESTION NUMBER 9

What do you think the qualities of a good team player are?

Remember the Royal Navy motto? 'The team works'. I have already made reference to the importance of teamwork during this guide and there is a possibility that you will be asked a question that relates to your ability to work as part of a team and also what you think the qualities of an effective team worker are. Whilst on board ship there is a high risk that things can go wrong. You are hundred's of miles away from land and any support from other ships could be hours away. If something serious goes wrong then you have to work very fast and professionally as part of a team in order to resolve the issue. Before you can work effectively as a team however you need to know what the main qualities of a competent team member include. Take a look at the following:

> An ability to interact and work with others, regardless of their age, sex, religion, sexual orientation, background, disability or appearance;

> Being able to communicate with everyone in the team and provide the appropriate level of support and encouragement;

> Being capable of carrying out tasks correctly, professionally and in accordance with guidelines and regulations;

> Being focused on the team's goal(s);

> Having a flexible attitude and approach to the task;

> Putting the needs of the team first before your own;

> Putting personal differences aside for the sake of the team;

> Being able to listen to others suggestions and contributions.

When responding to this type of question it would be an advantage if you could back up your response with an example of where you already work in a team. Take a look at the following sample response before creating your own based on your own experiences and ideas.

SAMPLE RESPONSE TO INTERVIEW QUESTION NUMBER 9

What do you think the qualities of a good team player are?

'A good team player must have many different qualities including an ability to listen carefully to a given brief. If you don't listen to the brief that is provided then you can't complete the task properly. In addition to listening carefully to the brief you must be able to communicate effectively with everyone in the team. As a Royal Navy Officer this will be even more important. As a team member and leader I will be responsible for supporting the other team members and also listening to other people's suggestions on how a task can be achieved. You also have to be able to work with anyone in the team regardless of their age, background, religion, sexual orientation, disability or appearance. You can't discriminate against anyone and if you do, then there is no place for you within that team. A good team player must also be able to carry out his or her job professionally and competently. When I say competently I mean correctly and in accordance with guidelines and training. You should also be focused on the team's goal and not be distracted by any external factors. Putting the needs of the team first is paramount. Finally a good team player must be flexible and be able to adapt to the changing requirements of the team.

I already have some experience of working in a team and I know how important it is to work hard at achieving the task. I have a job working in my local supermarket as a junior supervisor and every week we have a team briefing. During the team briefings it is my responsibility to inform the team what tasks need to be carried out as a priority. During one particular meeting I asked the team to clear a fire escape that had become blocked with cardboard boxes, debris and rubbish. In addition to this I also asked the team to come up with a plan to prevent it from happening again. Once I had briefed the team members we all set about the task carefully removing the rubbish. Once this was completed we then worked together in order to devise a plan to prevent it from happening again. Whilst it is important to delegate work as a leader, it is just as important to be able to work as part of that team, encouraging, supporting and communicating as you progress through the task.'

SAMPLE INTERVIEW QUESTION NUMBER 10

What do you do in your spare time?

Questions of this nature are designed to assess how effectively you use your spare time. If you are an inactive person who sits in watching television most days then you are less likely to adapt to the change in lifestyle the Navy will bring as opposed to if you are a fit, active and sporty type of person. Take a look at the following two lists which differentiate between positive ways to spend your spare time and negative ways.

Positive ways to spend your spare time

> Brisk walking, running, gym work, swimming, cycling, indoor rowing;

> Studying for exams or academic qualifications;

> Preparing for a goal or aspiration such as joining the Royal Navy;

> Team activities such as football, hockey, rugby etc;

> Outdoor activities such as mountaineering, orienteering, mountain biking or climbing;

> Charity or voluntary work.

Negative ways to spend your spare time

> Sitting at home watching television or playing computer games;

> Spending hours on social networking sites;

> Sitting on park benches or being on the streets doing nothing.

Now take a look at the following sample response to this question which will assist you in your preparation.

SAMPLE RESPONSE TO INTERVIEW QUESTION NUMBER 10

What do you do in your spare time?

'During my spare time I like to keep active, both physically and mentally. I enjoy visiting the gym three times a week and I have a structured workout that I try and vary every few months to keep my interest up. When I attend the gym I like to work out using light weights and I also enjoy using the indoor rower. I always try and beat my best time over a 2000 metre distance.

I'm also currently doing a weekly evening class in Judo, which is one of my hobbies. I haven't achieved any grades yet but I am taking my first one in a few weeks time. I'm also a member of the local Sea Cadets, which is an evening's commitment every week and the occasional weekend. Of course, I know when it is time to relax and usually do this by either listening to music or playing snooker with my friends but, overall, I'm quite an active person. I certainly don't like sitting around doing nothing. I understand that if I'm successful in joining the Navy then there will be lots to keep me occupied in the evenings, especially during my basic training.'

SAMPLE INTERVIEW QUESTION NUMBER 11

Can you tell me about any achievements you have experienced during your life so far?

Those people who can demonstrate a history of achievement during the Royal Navy interview are far more likely to pass the initial officer training course. Demonstrating a history of achievement already will work in your favour. Having achieved something in your life demonstrates that you have the ability to see things through to the end, something which is crucial to your career in the Navy as an officer. It also shows that you are motivated and determined to succeed.

Try to think of examples where you have succeeded or achieved something relevant in your life. Some good examples of achievements are as follows:

> Winning a trophy with a football or hockey team;

> GCSE's, A Levels, Degree's and other educational qualifications;

> Duke of Edinburgh's Awards;

> Being given responsibility at work or at school;

> Raising money for charity.

> Keeping physically fit and playing team sports.

SAMPLE RESPONSE TO INTERVIEW QUESTION NUMBER 11

Can you tell me about any achievements you have experienced during your life so far?

'Yes I can. So far in my life I have achieved quite a few things that I am proud

of. To begin with I achieved good grades whilst at school in both my GCSE's and A levels. I worked very hard to achieve my grades and I'm proud of them. At weekends I play rugby for a local team and I've achieved a number of things with them. Apart from winning the league last year we also held a charity match against the local Police rugby team. We managed to raise £500 for a local charity which was great achievement.

More recently I managed to achieve a huge increase in my fitness levels in preparation of the Pre Joining Fitness Test. Before I started my preparation I couldn't reach the minimum standard required but I have since worked vary hard and I can now easily pass the required target for my age group.'

SAMPLE INTERVIEW QUESTION NUMBER 12

What are your strengths and what are you good at?

This is a common interview question that is relatively easy to answer. The problem with it is that many people use the same response. It is quite an easy thing to tell the interviewer that you are dedicated and the right person for the job. However, it is a different thing backing it up with evidence!

If you are asked this type of question make sure you are positive during your response and show that you actually mean what you are saying. Then, back up the strengths you have mentioned with examples of when you have been something that you say you are. For example, if you tell the panel that you are a motivated person, back it up with an example in your life where you have achieved something through sheer motivation and determination.

SAMPLE RESPONSE TO INTERVIEW QUESTION NUMBER 12

What are your strengths and what are you good at?

'To begin with, I'm a determined person who likes to see things through to the end. For example, I recently ran a marathon for charity. I'd never done this kind of thing before and found it very hard work, but I made sure I completed the task. Another strength of mine is that I'm always looking for ways to improve myself. As an example, I have been preparing for the Navy Officer selection process by embarking on an evening class that will see me eventually achieve a Diploma in management Studies. Although I have a small amount of managerial and supervisory experience, I want to make sure that I am in the best position possible for becoming a competent Royal

Navy Officer. Finally, I would say that one of my biggest strengths is that I'm a great team player. I really enjoy working in a team environment and achieving things through a collaborative approach. For example, I play in a local rugby team and we recently won the league trophy for the first time since the club was established some 50 years ago.'

SAMPLE INTERVIEW QUESTION NUMBER 13

What are your weaknesses?

Now this is a difficult question to answer. We all have weaknesses and anyone who says they haven't, is probably not telling truth. However, you must be very careful how you respond to this question. Apart from being truthful you must also provide a weakness that you are working hard on to improve. You should also remember that you are joining a disciplined service that requires hard work, determination and a will to succeed. So, if you are the type of person who cannot get up in the morning and you keep making regular mistakes at work or at school, then the Royal Navy might not be for you.

The key to responding to this type of question is to be truthful but to also back it up with examples of what you are doing to improve your weakness. Take a look at the following example.

SAMPLE RESPONSE TO INTERVIEW QUESTION NUMBER 13

What are your weaknesses?

'My biggest is weakness is that sometimes I work too hard. Once I get in from my day job I am straight upstairs working on my computer, studying for a course I have undertaken. Whilst being hard working is a positive aspect to my character, I do need to learn to relax and take time out. I will never be a lazy person and I really do get a lot out of working, but I must take more time to relax as this will help me to perform better when I am at work.'

SAMPLE INTERVIEW QUESTION NUMBER 14

Why do you want to become an Officer? Why don't you become a Rating instead?

This type of question is designed to see if there are any genuine reasons why you have chosen to become an officer. Some applicants get carried away with the perceived glamour and status of the role, without putting any serious thought into why they actually want to become an officer. When preparing your response to this question you need to think about the skills and attributes that you have already gained that are relevant to the role of a Royal Navy Officer. You may already have some genuine reasons why you want to become an officer but please read the following sample response which will give you some good pointers when preparing your response.

SAMPLE RESPONSE TO INTERVIEW QUESTION NUMBER 14

Why do you want to become an Officer? Why don't you become a Rating instead?

'I have thought long and hard about applying to become a officer and I am fully certain that this is what I want to do. To begin with, I spent considerable time assessing my own qualities and attributes and I believe they would be most suited to that of an officer. I am hard working, tenacious, resolute, professional, driven and ambitious and feel that these qualities will allow me to eventually become a competent officer in the Royal Navy. In addition to my qualities I have already gained some experience in a supervisory role within my current job. I really enjoy the additional responsibility that this brings and would not thrive in a role that holds little or no responsibility. It is my ultimate goal to join the Royal Navy and serve as an officer. I am determined and resolute and believe that I would make an invaluable contribution to this elite service.'

SAMPLE INTERVIEW QUESTION NUMBER 15

What are the different ranks for both Royal Navy Officers and Ratings?

This question assesses your knowledge of the ranks within the Royal Navy. It is a simple question and one that should be relatively easy to respond to. Having an understanding of the different ranks for both commissioned and non-commissioned staff will be an obvious advantage for when you start your initial training. On the following page are the ranks within the Royal Navy for you to study:

RATINGS

Rating

Leading Rate

Petty Officer

Chief Petty Officer

Warrant Officer 2

Warrant Officer 1

OFFICERS

Midshipman

Sub-lieutenant

Lieutenant

Lieutenant- Commander

Commander

Captian

Commodore

Rear Admiral

Vice-Admiral

Admiral

Admiral of the Fleet

You may also decide to study the different markings for each rank prior to your interview. These can be viewed at the Royal Navy's website www.royalnavy.mod.uk.

FURTHER SAMPLE INTERVIEW QUESTIONS

Q16. Tell me about the basic training you will undergo as an officer?

Q17. What is the minimum service contract you will be required to sign as an officer?

Q18. What part of Naval Officer training would you find the hardest?

Q19. What have you been doing so far to prepare for the Admiralty Interview Board?

Q20. If you fail officer selection, would you consider joining as an officer?

FINAL INTERVIEW TIPS

Within this section of the guide I will provide you with some final tips that will help you prepare for the Royal Navy Officer filter interview. Remember that your success will very much depend on how prepared you are. Don't forget to work on your interview technique, carry out plenty of research and work on your responses to the interview questions.

> In the build up to the interview carry out plenty of targeted preparation work. Read your recruitment literature and spend time studying the Royal Navy website. Ask the AFCO recruitment advisor to provide you with further information about the officer training you'll undergo.

> Work on your interview technique and make sure you try out at least one mock interview. This involves getting your family or friends to sit you down and ask you the interview questions that are contained within this guide;

> When you receive your date for the interview make sure you turn up on time. Check your travel and parking arrangements the day before your interview. The last thing you need is to be late for your interview!

> Think carefully about what you are going to wear during the interview. I am not saying that you should go out and buy an expensive suit but I do recommend you make an effort to dress smartly. Having said that, if you do decide to wear a smart suit or formal outfit make sure it is clean and pressed. You can still look scruffy in a suit.

> Personal hygiene is all part and parcel of Royal Navy life. Don't attend the interview unwashed, dirty or fresh from the building site!

> When you walk into the interview room, stand up straight with your shoulders back. Project an image of confidence and be polite, courteous and respectful to the interviewer at all times;

> Don't sit down in the interview chair until invited to do so. This will display good manners;

> Whilst you are in the interview chair sit upright with your hands resting on your knees, palms facing downwards. It is OK to use your hands expressively, but don't overdo it;

> Don't slouch in the chair. At the end of each question readjust your position;

> Whilst responding to the interview questions make sure you speak up and be positive. You will need to demonstrate a level of motivation and enthusiasm during the interview;

> Go the extra mile and learn a little bit about the Royal Navy's history. When the panel ask you "What can you tell us about the Royal Navy?" you will be able to demonstrate that you have made an effort to look into their history as well as their modern day activities;

> Ask positive questions at the end of the interview. Don't ask questions such as "How much leave will I get?" or "How often do I get paid?"

> If you are unsure about a question try not to 'waffle'. If you do not know the answer, then it is OK to say so. Move on to the next question and put it behind you.

> Finally, believe in yourself and be confident.

CHAPTER 3 THE AIB SCORING CRITERIA

Before I go onto explain the scoring criteria, let us first of all take a look at some of the competencies required to successfully pass the Royal Navy Officer initial training course at Britannia Royal Naval College (BRNC).

COMPETENCIES REQUIRED FOR SUCCESS DURING INITIAL OFFICER TRAINING

Interpersonal Competencies

Communicating effectively	Is able to communicate accurately and effectively both orally and in writing.
Teamwork	Is able to work with others to achieve common goals.
Influencing	Can influence others to follow a certain course of action.

Problem Solving Competencies

Appreciation	Comprehends, identifies, extracts and assimilates information from a range of sources, quickly and accurately.
Reasoning	Thinks logically, practically and coherently to produce a successful or reasonable solution, quickly and accurately.
Organisation	Determines priorities and allocates resources effectively and efficiently to a task(s).
Capacity	Holds and processes multiple inputs whilst maintaining task performance.

Character Competencies

Decisiveness	Makes sound appropriate decisions within time-scale demanded by the situation.
Self-motivation	Demonstrates a high level of commitment and interest to tasks.
Self-analysis	Monitors and objectively analyses own performance
Integrity	Behaviour is guided by principles, morals and ethics appropriate to service life. Adheres to rules and regulations specific to the Royal Navy.

Now that we understand some of the competencies that are required to pass Royal Navy Initial Officer Training, we can explore the type of qualities the assessors will be looking for during the Admiralty Interview Board.

EXAMPLES OF COMPETENCIES ASSESSED DURING THE ADMIRALTY INTERVIEW BOARD

Example competency	Description
Communication	• Delivers communication in a concise and effective manner, both written and orally. • Listens to others suggestions. • Contributes when appropriate. • Understands the situation/ discussion.
Teamwork	• Is able to work with others in order to achieve a task or goal. • Puts in plenty of effort. • Treats others appropriately. • Supports other team members. • Communicates with the team. • Encourages the team.
Influencing	• Has considerable impact on others. • Can persuade and direct others.
Problem Solving	• Can judge certain situations. • Is flexible. • Is decisive. • Can come up with solutions to most problems.
Confidence and Resilience	• Self assured. • Is composed and calm. • Acts with a sense of urgency when required. • Can be assertive is required. • Perseveres. • Determined. • Resolute.

WHEN ARE THE COMPETENCIES ASSESSED?

Each of the qualities will be assessed during every stage of the AIB, although some more than others. For example, you will be assessed on your influencing capabilities considerably during the planning exercise and your teamwork skills during the Practical Leadership Task (PLT) when you are not in command.

You can begin to understand now why it is not important to find out what tasks you are going to undertake during the AIB. What is important is how you perform and behave in accordance with the Personal Qualities and the Core Competencies being assessed.

CHAPTER 4
ADMIRALTY INTERVIEW BOARD RUNNING ORDER AND TIPS

During this brief chapter I will provide you with a sample running order for the Admiralty Interview Board. It will give you a basic idea of what you will go through during your stay at the BRNC.

I have also provided you with a number of useful tips to help you prepare for each element.

THE BIOGRAPHICAL QUESTIONNAIRE

Before you arrive at the AIB you will be sent a questionnaire to complete. This helps the Royal Navy make an initial assessment about you. Therefore, it is important that you complete the form as fully and accurately as possible. It is your chance to blow your own trumpet. Please see a previous section of this guide for sample responses to some of the questions.

THE FIRST EVENING (DAY ONE)

This is when you will report to the candidates' reception and find out about where you will be living over the two days. Remember to hand in your completed biographical questionnaire. My advice is to dress smart for the AIB. You do not have to invest in an expensive designer suit, but do make the effort to look smart and informal. Personal hygiene is also very important.

THE FIRST FULL DAY (DAY TWO)

You will sit:

> A 20-minute verbal reasoning test designed to demonstrate your general reasoning and ability with words;

> A 13-minute non-verbal reasoning test, again measuring your reasoning power, but this time without the emphasis on verbal skills;

> A 25-minute numerical test covering numerical fluency, reasoning and statistics;

> A 15-minute speed and accuracy test, measuring your concentration and mental agility;

> A 15-minute spatial orientation test, involving directions, relative positions and movement;

> A short general service knowledge test to provide the Board with an indication of your research into the Royal Navy.

I have provided you with a number of useful practice materials which you can download at the following link:

RoyalNavyOfficerResources.co.uk

ESSAY

Follow the tests you will be given 45 minutes to write about a subject chosen from a list of four topics. This assessment will assess your written communication skills. During the essay you are assessed against:

- Overall construction (e.g. paragraphing);
- Sentence construction;
- Style;

- Relevance of points and arguments;
- Vocabulary;
- Impact;
- Legibility and spelling.

TIPS FOR CREATING AN EFFECTIVE ESSAY

Tip 1

For the introduction, write the thesis statement and give some background information. The thesis statement is put into the essay introduction and it should reveal your point of view on the matter, or position you intend to support in your paper.

Tip 2

Develop each supporting paragraph and make sure to follow the correct format.

Tip 3

Write clear and simple sentences to express your meaning. Concentrate on correct grammar, punctuation and spelling. If you are unsure how to spell a specific word, avoid using it!

Tip 4

Focus on the main idea of your essay.

Tip 5

Consider using a well structured format for your essay such as:

Beginning – Include the thesis statement and background information.

Middle –This will be the main part of the essay and will include your argument, the reasons for it and any supporting evidence or information.

End – Conclude and summarise. Make sure your conclusion actually concludes something and doesn't just leave you sitting on the fence, or the assessor unsure of what your actual point was.

In order to prepare for the essay, try writing one on any of the following topics:

SAMPLE ESSAY TOPIC 1

Politicians too often base their decisions on what will please the voters, not on what is best for the country.

SAMPLE ESSAY TOPIC 2

Wealthy politicians cannot offer fair representation to all the people.

SAMPLE ESSAY TOPIC 3

In a free society, laws must be subject to change.

SAMPLE ESSAY TOPIC 4

An understanding of the past is necessary for solving the problems of the present.

SAMPLE ESSAY TOPIC 5

Education comes not from books but from practical experience.

SAMPLE ESSAY TOPIC 6

Would National ID cards help prevent terrorism?

SAMPLE ESSAY TOPIC 7

Does immigration benefit the country?

SAMPLE ESSAY TOPIC 8

What will help curb gun and knife crime in the UK?

SAMPLE ESSAY TOPIC 9

Would National Service rehabilitate criminals?

FITNESS ASSESSMENT

In the afternoon of the second day you will complete a multi-stage fitness test (commonly known as the bleep test). This is not a pass or fail test but you need to put in maximum effort and your performance will be graded. You can obtain a copy of the test at www.how2become.co.uk.

THE FINAL DAY (DAY THREE)

PRACTICAL LEADERSHIP TASK (PLT)

Working in teams in the gym you are required to solve a practical problem, put a plan into action and respond to emerging difficulties. The task is designed to test your teamwork and leadership ability, your verbal powers of communication, and your resilience and strength of character.

Tips

- Be very supportive of your team.
- Be in control when you are the person in command.
- Acknowledge other's suggestions, but always be in control.
- Don't panic. It is OK to ask for suggestions.
- Think outside of the box. If an object provided is of no use to you, don't use it!

PLANNING EXERCISE

You will be provided with a written brief, containing details of a fictitious scenario. You will then have just 15 minutes to study the brief. Once the 15 minutes is up, the assessors will then introduce a problem into the scenario setting. You will then have 15 minutes to discuss possible solutions with your group and reach an agreed plan. You will then be required to present your agreed plan to the Board. Each person in the group will then be questioned in turn to examine their grasp of the situation.

Tips

- This is probably one of the hardest elements of AIB. It is crucial that you are competent in the use of Speed, Distance and Time. Please visit the Planning Exercise section of this guide which will assist you during your preparation.
- Read the scenario thoroughly! Do not skim through it as you will miss important elements.

- Be vocal and active during the group discussion stage of the exercise. Remember the important competency of 'influencing'.
- Explain your point of view and why your plan works.
- Don't dismiss others comments directly out of hand.
- Practice by carrying out plenty of Speed, distance and time questions (SDT). In addition to writing down SDT calculations, you should also get someone to fire questions at you. This is far harder than sitting down and working out the answers but it will be more beneficial to you during the AIB.
- Practice SDT questions at the following website: SpeedDistanceTime.info

COMPETENCY BASED INTERVIEW

The competency based interview lasts for approximately 30 minutes. Whilst I have provided you with an entire section dedicated to this interview, here's a few important tips to help you prepare:

1. During your preparation, think about times when you have already been a leader or supervisor. If you have no experience in this area then it would be a good idea to go and get some.

2. Think of times when you have organised something in your life. Write down the process that you followed from beginning to end.

3. Be able to provide examples of where you have been in a team and shown courage.

4. The assessors will ask you why you want to join the Royal Navy, your understanding of your chosen specialisation and your hopes and aspirations. They will also expect you to demonstrate your wider knowledge about the Royal Navy, and in particular to find out if it extends beyond a simple reading of the leaflets that they provide.

5. In the build up to the AIB, live and breathe the Royal Navy. If you are applying to become a pilot then visit an Air Base and also consider visiting the Fleet Air Arm museum which is based at RNAS Yeovilton. Visit www.FleetAirArm.com for more details.

6. Be competent in current affairs before you attend the AIB. See the later chapter that relates to the AIB interview for more tips, advice and a host of sample questions.

THE RESULT

The Royal Navy will normally tell you your results individually in the afternoon of the last day. If unsuccessful, you will be free to leave. However, if you have passed, you will need to complete a medical examination.

Success at the AIB does not guarantee entry into training. All successful candidates are placed in order of merit and the final selection will depend on the number of vacancies available and the number of successful candidates who reach the required medical and educational standards.

CHAPTER 5 THE PRACTICAL LEADERSHIP TASK (PLT)

During the Admiralty Interview Board you will be required to undertake a Practical Leadership Task or PLT as it is otherwise called. The PLT is usually carried out in a gym/hangar type setting and will incorporate come kind of obstacle course. During the PLT you will be required to:

i) Be part of the team when it is not your turn to lead.

ii) Act as the leader of a task during a specific task that you must resolve.

When acting as the leader it will be your responsibility to brief the team, lead them and solve a specific problem. When you are not the person leading you will need to act as a competent team player and assist the team in achieving its goal(s).

Let's now take a look at how you can achieve higher marks during the PLT. I will break the information down into two sections, one section for when you are acting as part of the team and one section when you are the designated leader.

WHEN ACTING AS A TEAM MEMBER

When acting as a team member you will still be assessed. Team work is an essential part of Royal Naval life, so make sure you work hard to complete the task and assist the designated leader. You should get stuck in, come up with suggestions, listen to the leader, support other team members and shout words of encouragement.

WHEN ACTING AS THE DESIGNATED LEADER

This is obviously the most important part of the PLT. It is your chance to shine as the leader so take stock of the following components and try to implement them into your turn as the leader.

Component 1 – Brief

You will be provided with a brief at the beginning of the task. It will be your responsibility to read the brief carefully, brief the members of your team and come up with a solution to the problem. Listen to the brief very carefully and communicate every element of it to the rest of your team.

Component 2 – Plan

Every team that is working towards a common goal should have a plan in place. If you don't have a plan, how are you going to achieve the task in hand? The way to compile a successful plan is to ask the team if they have any ideas on how the task could be achieved. You may however already have ideas of your own for how the problem could be solved. If so, brief your team and then go all out to achieve the task.

Component 3 – Time

It is important that any team working towards a common goal is aware of the time constraints. Make sure everyone is aware of the time and keep checking it regularly, if the facility exists. As the designated leader you may decide to appoint a dedicated timekeeper. It is crucial that you and your team act with a sense of urgency at all times.

Component 4 – Communication

This is probably the most important component of any team task. Communication means talking to, and listening to, the other members of the team. Get this part wrong and the task is guaranteed to fail. You should communicate with your team constantly.

Component 5 – Allocation of tasks

Everybody in the team will have different 'strengths'. You should try to find out who is good at what, and then allocate tasks accordingly. For example, if the task requires heavy lifting, find out who has the most strength in your team. If there are knots to be tied, is there anyone in your team capable of doing this? The phrase 'round pegs in round holes' springs to mind!

Component 6 – Support

It is the duty of every team member to support the other members of the team. You should shout words of encouragement to your team members. Whilst this may feel uncomfortable to some, if you fail to do it, you will score lower than you would otherwise. Here are a few suggestions:

"This is great work team, keep going!"

"Is everyone in the team OK? Let me know if there are any problems"

"Fantastic effort team, there's not too far to go now!"

At the end of the PLT, make sure you congratulate your team on their efforts – this is important. Go round and speak to everyone, pat them on the back and be vocally supportive of your team.

Component 7 – URGENCY!

Regardless of how long you have to complete the task, urgency is a must.

Now let's take a look at a number of tips that will help you to brief your team when you are the designated leader.

BRIEFING THE TEAM

Once you have received the brief from the assessing officer you will have a short period of time to come up with a plan in order to achieve the task. Here is an excellent format to follow when briefing any team in a command situation:

SMEAC

SITUATION – explain what the situation is.

"OK, gather around team and pay attention whilst I explain the situation. Our task today is to…"

MISSION – once you have explained the situation, tell the team what the mission is.

"Our mission is to..."

EXECUTION – tell your team how you are going to achieve the task including the allocation of tasks (plan).

"We will achieve the task by carrying out XYZ."

ASKING QUESTIONS – ask your team if anyone has any questions.

"Is the brief clear team? Does anyone have any questions?"

CHECK FOR UNDERSTANDING – check to see that your team fully understands what is expected from them.

"Is everyone clear of the team task and their role within the team?"

I have used SMEAC many times in the past during training exercises and also during firefighting operations. It provides a degree of organisation to any team and I would recommend that you learn it and use it during the command task when you are the person in charge.

OK, here's a few final tips to assist you during the PLT, both when you are a designated leader and team member.

Tip 1

When you are not the person in charge, be an effective team leader. Help out as much as possible and get stuck in! You may also wish to shout words of encouragement to the other members of the team.

"Let's keep going everyone, were doing a great job here."

Tip 2

When you are the allocated person in charge, take control of your team.

"OK everyone, gather around and pay attention to the following brief..."

Tip 3

Be supportive of your team members and get involved when necessary.

Tip 4

When briefing the team, consider using SMEAC.

Tip 5

If things start to go wrong, do not panic. Remain clam and in control. Keep going until the end and try your absolute hardest to complete the task. At the end of the task, whether it has been successful or not, thank your team for their efforts.

Tip 6

Keep an eye on safety. You are the person in charge and therefore responsible for safety.

CHAPTER 6
PREPARING FOR THE PLANNING EXERCISE

PLANNING EXERCISE

You will most probably find this element of the AIB the toughest. Before we look at how you can prepare effectively, here's an explanation as to what is involved.

INDIVIDUAL STUDY TIME

Each person will be provided with a copy of the brief/setting. You will then have just 15 minutes to sit in silence and read the scenario. It is important that you read everything carefully. Do not miss out any of the scenario as this could hinder you during the group discussion phase and questioning by the assessors. If you miss out anything, the assessors will pick up on it.

GROUP DISCUSSION

Once the 15 minute period is complete you will then have a period of time to discuss the scenario, and how you intend to approach it, with the other candidates in your group. During this stage make sure you are vocal and active in the construction of the plan – this is VERY important. Do not be afraid to make suggestions and if you have the confidence in your own plan, try and influence the other members of the group. Pay attention at all times, be involved and never dismiss someone's suggestions directly out of hand.

It is crucial that you are competent in the use of Speed, Distance and Time before you attend the AIB. My advice is simple:

> Practice SDT questions everyday in the build up to the AIB. You can obtain free SDT questions at the website www.SpeedDistanceTime.info. Although this website is primarily for RAF Officer candidates, it is perfect for those people who are attending the AIB.

>You should also practice SDT questions by having someone fire questions at you. This is a lot harder than working them out with a pen and paper!

Finally, be competent in the use of the 24 hour clock. The assessing officer's will expect you to use it when answering their questions.

TOP TIPS FOR SCORING HIGH DURING THE PLANNING EXERCISE

- Demonstrate strength of character
- Don't give in, even if things are going wrong
- Support your decision and consider all eventualities
- Improve general arithmetic and be competent in the use of speed, distance and time (SDT)
- Be able to calculate SDT questions in your head, as well as being able to write them down. You can practice by getting a member of your family to ask you a series of SDT questions. This is great practice as you will be under pressure to answer the questions without the use of a calculator, pen and paper.
- Keep an eye on the time. You need to come up with a solution to the problem.
- Be alert and quick to respond to questions.
- Never lie when answering questions from the assessors, they will see straight through it. If you do not know the answer to a question, then just say so.

- Always remain calm. The questioning at the end of the exercise is designed to be tough and assess how well you cope under pressure.

SPEED, DISTANCE AND TIME

Accuracy and agility in speed, distance, and time calculations will help you perform well during the Royal Navy Officer selection process. The following information will assist you in understanding how to tackle these types of question.

When trying to solve these problems it is important to consider three variables: speed, distance and time. Try not to get too worried as two of these variables will always be known. The easiest way to solve these equations is to use the following formulas:

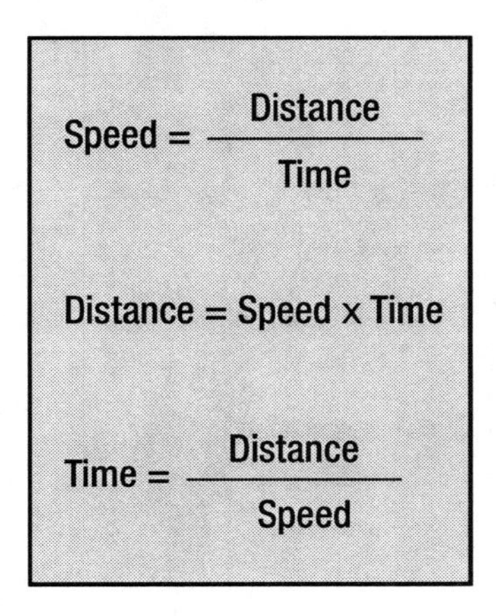

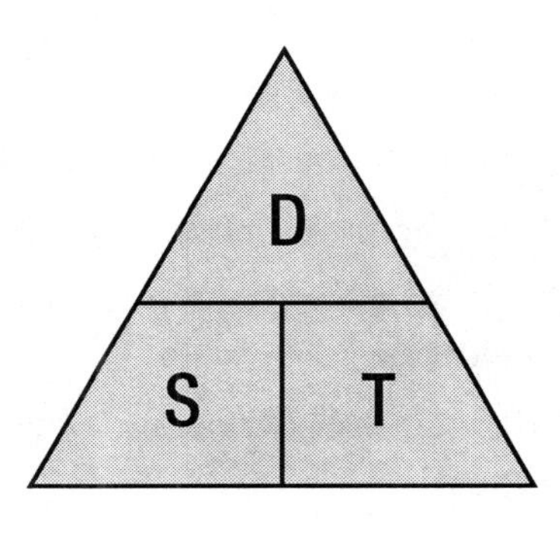

The triangular diagram above is ideal for helping you to remember the formula. Simply place your finger over the variable you are trying to discover, you will then see the equation required.

For example if you wanted to obtain the time, placing your finger on 'T' would show that you would need to *divide* distance (D) by speed (S).

Let's now work through some examples:

1. A train travels 60 miles in 3 hours. What is the train's speed?

Formula: Speed = distance ÷ time

Speed = 60 ÷ 3 = 20 mph

2. A car is travelling at 30 mph for 70 minutes. What is the distance travelled?

With this problem it is important to remember to work in minutes!

So, 30 mph = 0.5 miles per minute (30 ÷ 60)

70 (minutes) × 0.5 = 35 miles

You can use the formula but you need to convert the minutes into hours and remember that 0.1 = 1/10 of 60 minutes:

Formula: Distance = speed × time

Distance = 30 × 1.1666r (1 hour 10 mins) = 35

3. A tank is driving at 48 mph over 60 miles. How long was it driving for?

Formula: Time =distance ÷ speed

Time = 60 ÷ 48 = 1 hour 15 minutes

Take these steps

I. You know that 48 mph = 48 miles in 60 minutes.

II. The difference between 60 and 48 is 12, which is ¼ of 48.

III. You can then take ¼ of 60, which gives 15 minutes, and add that to 60 minutes = 75 minutes.

IV. Then convert to hours = 1 hour 15 minutes for the answer!

OR

Take these steps

I. You know that 48 mph = 0.8 miles per minute.

II. 60 ÷ 0.8 = 75 minutes.

III. Convert into hours = 1 hour 15 minutes.

Once you understand how to calculate speed, distance and time, take your time to work through the 30 sample test questions that follow.

SAMPLE SPEED, DISTANCE AND TIME TEST QUESTIONS

(Give all distances and speeds in whole numbers)

Question 1

You are travelling at 28mph for 75 minutes. How far do you travel?

Answer ☐

Question 2

You travel 15 miles in half an hour. What speed are you travelling at?

Answer ☐

Question 3

You travel 33 miles at a constant speed of 55mph. How long are you travelling for?

Answer ☐

Question 4

You are travelling at 75 mph for 1 and half hours. How far do you travel?

Answer ☐

Question 5

You travel 61 miles in 1 hour and 5 minutes. What speed are you travelling at?

Answer ☐

Question 6

You travel 90 miles at a constant speed of 30 mph. How long are you travelling for?

Answer ☐

Question 7

You are travelling at 70mph for 125 minutes. How far do you travel?

Answer ☐

Question 8

You travel 2.5 miles in 5 minutes. What speed are you travelling at?

Answer [ ]

Question 9

You travel 75 miles at a constant speed of 45mph. How long are you travelling for?

Answer [ ]

Question 10

You are travelling at 59 mph for quarter of an hour. How far do you travel?

Answer [ ]

Question 11

You travel 325 miles in 4 hours and 6 minutes. What speed are you travelling at?

Answer [ ]

Question 12

You travel 38 miles at 45 mph. How long are you travelling for?

Answer [ ]

Question 13

You are travelling at 80 mph for 15 minutes. How far do you travel?

Answer [ ]

Question 14

You travel 63 miles in 56 minutes. What speed are you travelling at?

Answer [ ]

Question 15

You travel 18 miles at 50 mph. How long are you travelling for?

Answer ☐

Question 16

You are travelling at 65 mph for one hour and 10 minutes. How far do you travel?

Answer ☐

Question 17

You travel 120 miles in two hours. What speed are you travelling at?

Answer ☐

Question 18

You travel 80 miles at 50 mph. How long are you travelling for?

Answer ☐

Question 19

You are travelling at 40 mph for half an hour. How far do you travel?

Answer ☐

Question 20

You travel 80 miles in 1 ¾ of an hour. What speed are you travelling at?

Answer ☐

Question 21

You travel 35 miles at 70 mph. How long are you travelling for?

Answer ☐

Question 22

You are travelling at 15 mph for 8 minutes. How far do you travel?

Answer [ ]

Question 23

You travel 16 miles in quarter of an hour. What speed are you travelling at?

Answer [ ]

Question 24

You travel 60 miles at 55 mph. How long are you travelling for?

Answer [ ]

Question 25

You are travelling at 30 mph for 10 minutes. How far do you travel?

Answer [ ]

Question 26

You travel 75 miles in one and half hours. What speed are you travelling at?

Answer [ ]

Question 27

You travel 1 mile at 60 mph. How long are you travelling for?

Answer [ ]

Question 28

You are travelling at 50 mph for 2 and half hours. How far do you travel?

Answer [ ]

Question 29

You travel 100 miles in 1 hour and 55 minutes. What speed are you travelling at?

Answer [ ]

Question 30

You travel 600 miles at 80 mph. How long are you travelling for?

Answer ☐

ANSWERS TO SPEED, DISTANCE AND TIME TEST

1. 35 miles
2. 30 mph
3. 36 mins
4. 112.5 miles
5. 56 mph
6. 3 hours
7. 146 miles
8. 30 mph
9. 1hour 40 minutes
10. 15 miles
11. 79 mph
12. 51 mins
13. 20 miles
14. 68 mph
15. 21 minutes and 30 seconds
16. 76 miles
17. 60mph
18. 1 hour 36 mins
19. 20 miles
20. 46mph
21. 30 mins
22. 2 miles
23. 64mph
24. 1 hour 5 mins
25. 5 miles
26. 50mph
27. 1 minute
28. 125 miles
29. 52 mph
30. 7 hours 30 minutes

On the following pages I have provided you with a sample planning exercise for you to try. Give it a go and see how you get on. There is no time limit for this sample exercise.

PLANNING EXERCISE - SEASIDE MISSION

You are the duty officer in charge at the Royal National Lifeboat Institution's (RNLI) rescue centre at FLITTERBY. The FLITTERBY lifeboat is currently involved in rescuing some sailors from a drifting yacht in the Irish Sea.

It is exactly 10:00 am and the coxswain of the lifeboat has just radioed the following message to you:

"One of the sailors we have taken off from the sinking yacht is desperately ill and must have a blood transfusion as soon as possible. I have just been talking, by radio, to the Accident & Emergency (A&E) staff at ASHBY hospital and they will be standing-by to receive him but have pointed out that every minute counts. Make sure the RNLI's ambulance (a specially adapted estate car) is ready to take him to the hospital as soon as we arrive at the jetty. I cannot give you an exact time of arrival, but it will not be before 10:20 hours, or later than 10:45 hours. Once we are tied up, it will take us 5 minutes to get him from the boat into the ambulance. It will be up to you to get him from the jetty to the A&E dept with the utmost urgency."

You study the map and recollect that there are 3 ways to get to hospital, each with advantages and disadvantages:

1. The route via the gate bridge is subject to delays as the crossings are controlled and the bridge is only open 3 times per hour for 12 minutes. The bridge is open at 10 minutes past, 30 minutes past and 10 minutes to the hour. The journey across the gate bridge will take you 10 minutes. The B120 is twisty and a maximum average speed could be no greater than 40 mph.

2. The route through the centre of ASHBY on the A424 is further but although it should be possible to average 40 mph out of town, once inside the central congestion zone, heavy traffic and narrow streets means no more than 5 mph can be averaged for the 10 miles through the walled part of the town. The one limitation from using the A424 is that from 11:00 hrs onwards the central congestion zone is very dense and traffic is at a standstill.

3. The new A11 by-pass is dual carriage and passes the hospital but, although the longest route, will allow averages of 70 mph to be achieved. It is possible to reach the A11 from FLITTERBY in 10 mins.

You warn the duty driver to stand-by. Unfortunately, you cannot alert the local police on the telephone to make any special arrangements, so there is no way of interrupting the steady but reliable timetable of the gate bridge. The duty officer at nearby RAF Valley tells you the Search and Rescue helicopter is unavailable as it is on a mission rescuing someone from an oil rig miles out to sea.

Your aim is to transport the sailor to the hospital in the quickest time possible.

Question 1

What is the earliest time that the sailor will arrive at RNLI Flitterby?

Answer [ ]

Question 2

What is the latest time the sailor will arrive at RNLI Flitterby?

Answer [ ]

Question 3

How long in minutes will it take you to get from RNLI Flitterby to the A11 junction?

Answer [ ]

Question 4

Based on the sailor arriving at RNLI Flitterby at the latest time possible, which route do you choose and why?

Question 5

Based on the sailor arriving at RNLI Flitterby at the earliest time possible, which route do you choose and why?

NOTE - You are to calculate the total journey times for each of the 3 different routes using Speed, Distance and Time calculations.

YOUR CALCULATIONS

Remember:

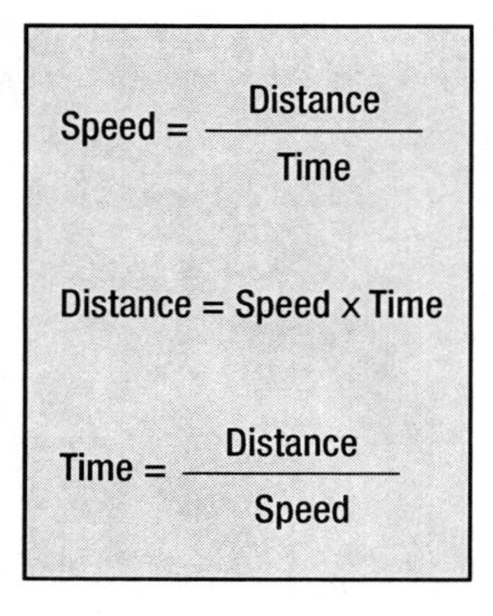

$$\text{Speed} = \frac{\text{Distance}}{\text{Time}}$$

$$\text{Distance} = \text{Speed} \times \text{Time}$$

$$\text{Time} = \frac{\text{Distance}}{\text{Speed}}$$

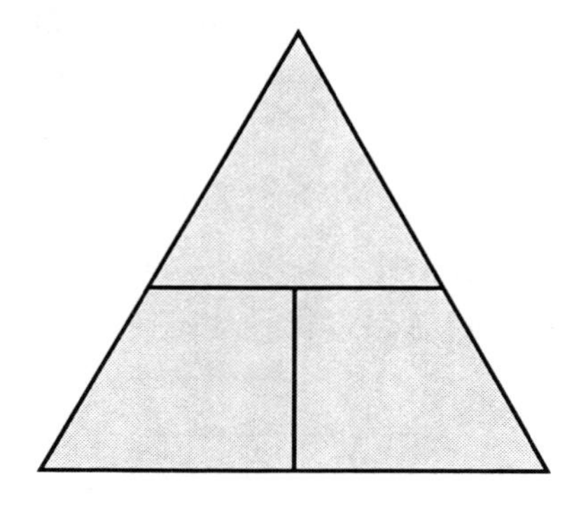

SEASIDE MISSION SKETCH

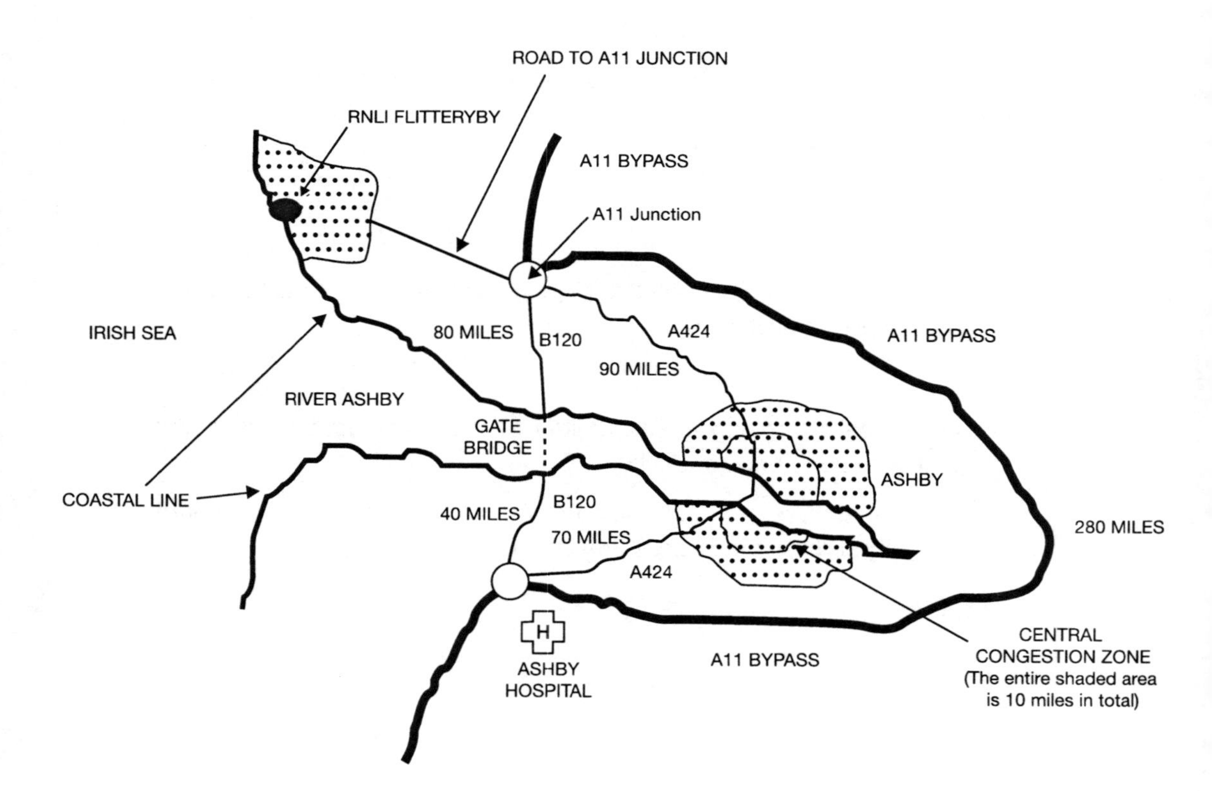

ANSWERS TO QUESTIONS

Question 1

How long in minutes will it take you to get from RNLI Flitterby to the A11 junction?

ANSWER: 10 minutes

Question 2

Based on the sailor arriving at Flitterby at the earliest time possible, what time will you reach the Hospital if you choose route 1?

The sailor arrives at Flitterby at 10:20hrs. It takes 5 minutes to load him into the ambulance which brings the time to 10:25hrs. It takes 10 minutes to get to the A11 junction which brings the time to 10:35hrs.

Travelling route 1, it is a total of 80 miles to the Gate Bridge. We are able to travel at a maximum speed of 40mph. To find out the time it takes to travel this distance we need to use the following calculation:

Time = Distance / Speed
Time = 80 / 40

ANSWER: 2 hours

We now know that we will arrive at the Gate Bridge at 12:35hrs. From the information provided we know that the Gate Bridge is open 3 times per hour for 12 minutes. The bridge is open at 10 minutes past, 30 minutes past and 10 minutes to the hour.

The bridge is already open when we arrive at 12:35 hours; therefore we are able to cross straight away. The journey across the gate bridge takes us 10 minutes, which means that we will arrive on the other side at 12:45hrs.

We now have to make the final journey along the B120 towards the hospital. The distance is 40 miles in total and we can travel at a maximum speed of 40 miles per hour. In order to calculate the time we need to use the following calculation:

Time = Distance / Speed
Time = 40 / 40

Answer = 1 hour

ANSWER: Arrive at the hospital at 13:45hrs.

Question 3

Based on the sailor arriving at Flitterby at the latest time possible, what time will you reach the Hospital if you choose route 3?

The sailor arrives at Flitterby at 10:45hrs. It takes 5 minutes to load him into the ambulance which brings the time to 10:50hrs. It takes 10 minutes to get to the A11 junction which brings the time to 11:00hrs.

Travelling along route 3 we know that we can achieve a maximum speed of 70 miles per hour. In order to work out the total time it will take us to reach the hospital we need to use the following calculation:

Time = Distance / Speed
Time = 280 / 70
Answer = 4 hours

ANSWER: Arrive at the hospital will be 15:00hrs.

Question 4

Based on the sailor arriving at Flitterby at the latest time possible, what time will you reach the Hospital if you choose route 1?

The sailor arrives at Flitterby at 10:45hrs. It takes 5 minutes to load him into the ambulance which brings the time to 10:50hrs. It takes 10 minutes to get to the A11 junction which brings the time to 11:00hrs.

Travelling route 1, it is a total of 80 miles to the Gate Bridge. We are able to travel at a maximum speed of 40mph. To find out the time it takes to travel this distance we need to use the following calculation:

Time = Distance / Speed
Time = 80 / 40
Answer = 2 hours

We now know that we will arrive at the Gate Bridge at 13:00hrs. From the information provided we know that the Gate Bridge is open 3 times per hour for 12 minutes. The bridge is open at 10 minutes past, 30 minutes past and 10 minutes to the hour.

The bridge is still open when we arrive at 13:00 hours; therefore we are able to cross straight away. The journey across the gate bridge takes us 10 minutes, which means that we will arrive on the other side at 13:10hrs.

We now have to make the final journey along the B120 towards the hospital.

The distance is 40 miles in total and we can travel at a maximum speed of 40 miles per hour. In order to calculate the time we need to use the following calculation:

Time = Distance / Speed
Time = 40 / 40
Answer = 1 hour

ANSWER: Arrive at the hospital at 14:10hrs.

Question 5

Based on the sailor arriving at Flitterby at the earliest time possible, what time will you reach the Hospital if you choose route 2?

The sailor arrives at Flitterby at 10:20hrs. It takes 5 minutes to load him into the ambulance which brings the time to 10:25hrs. It takes 10 minutes to get to the A11 junction which brings the time to 10:35hrs.

We know that the distance from the A11 junction to the edge of the congestion zone is a total of 90 miles. We also know that the distance from the other side of the congestion zone to the hospital along the A424 is a total of 70 miles. Therefore we can add these two distances together to get a total distance (minus the congestion zone area) of 160 miles. In order to work out the time it takes to travel this distance we need to use the following calculation:

Time = Distance / Speed
Time = 160 / 40
Answer = 4 hours

We now need to work out the time it will take us to travel through the congestion zone. We know from the map that the distance inside the congestion zone is a total of 10 miles. We can only travel at a maximum speed of 5mph; therefore the calculation used to find out the total time it takes to travel through the congestion zone is as follows:

Time = Distance / Speed
Time = 10 / 5
Answer = 2 hours

All we need to do now is add the two travelling times together to reach a total of 6 hours travelling time.

ANSWER: Arrive at the hospital at 16:35hrs

CHAPTER 7

HOW TO PASS THE ADMIRALTY INTERVIEW BOARD INTERVIEW

During this section of the guide I will provide you with a number of sample interview questions and advice on how to answer them. Whilst some of the questions will appear to be easy to answer, it is still important that we cover them, in order to ensure that you are fully prepared for you AIB. I also recommend that you re-visit the AFCO filter interview section of the guide as some of the questions asked may be duplicated.

I have divided the sample questions into various different sections to assist you during your preparation.

Section 1 - Personal questions

Q. When and where were you born?

Q. Where are you living now and who are you living with?

Q. Where else have you lived apart from with your parents?

Q. Describe your home life to me?

Q. What was your life like growing up?

TIPS – Questions that relate to your home life are designed to assess how stable you are as person, whether or not you have any responsibilities at home, whether you are generally a happy person and also what you have learnt from life's experiences to date.

> Know key dates of where you have lived.

> Try and provide examples of where you have moved around. This demonstrates that you are flexible and adaptable when the need arises.

> It is preferable that your home life is stable.

> The more responsibilities you have at home, such as washing, ironing, cleaning, financial responsibilities etc, the better.

> If you have lived with other people, apart from your immediate family, tell them so. Remember – as a Royal Navy Officer you will be living with men and women of different ages etc.

Education

Education

Q. How many schools have you attended and what years did you attend them?

Q. What did you think about your teachers?

Q. Tell me about your exam results; did you achieve the grades you wanted?

Q. Could you have worked harder whilst at school?

TIPS: although these are relatively easy questions to respond to, ones that relate to your exam results and how hard you worked whilst at school could catch you out. You have to be honest about your results. If they were not up to the standard that you expected, have a valid reason why. Never be disrespectful of your teachers or the educational system. Remember that you are applying to join a disciplined service.

School/college

Q. Did you learn anything from other students?

Q. Did you have any responsibilities whilst at school or college?

Q. What sports did you participate in whilst at school or college?

Q. What clubs or societies were you a member of?

Q. Do you have the Duke of Edinburgh or similar awards?

Q. Where did you travel with school?

Q. Did you have any gaps in your education?

TIPS: if you did have any gaps in your education, it is better to say that you used the time wisely. Maybe you went travelling around the world in order to gain new experiences and cultures, or maybe you wanted to take time out from your studies to take on a work related role or even a charity role. Whatever you do, do not say that you did nothing with your time off. If you went travelling, what did you gain from the experience?

Whilst at school or college it would be an advantage if you had some level of responsibility. For example, maybe you were a prefect or head of year, or maybe you were the captain of a sports team. You are applying to become an officer, which effectively means you are going to be a manager and a leader. Having some previous experience of these important roles will be an advantage. If you haven't had any responsibilities in your life to date, how do you know that you'll be a good leader or manager in the Royal Navy?

Outside interests and hobbies

Q. What sports are you currently engaged in?

Q. What sporting achievements have you gained?

Q. Have you been part of any youth organisations such as the Scouts or Guides?

Q. Describe your hobbies and interests?

Q. Are you currently employed either full-time or part-time?

Q. What did you used to do during your school holidays?

Q. Have you ever travelled? If so, where and when did you go and what did you gain from the experience(s)?

Q. What are you future ambitions or plans?

TIPS: It is imperative that you demonstrate during the interview that you are an active person. If you sit at home all evening on your computer, playing games and surfing the net, then you are probably not the type of person the Royal Navy are looking for. Demonstrate to the interviewer that you are active, a team player and have hobbies and interests that challenge you both mentally and physically.

Employment

Q. What jobs have you had to date?

Q. What responsibilities did you have during each job?

Q. Why did you leave each job?

Q. Did you complete any courses or gain any qualifications during each job?

Q. Who did you have to communicate with in each job?

Q. Were you part of a team or did you work alone?

Q. What were your appraisals like?

TIPS: If you have no experience in a work related role to date, how do you know that you will be a good employee for the Royal Navy? Make sure you have some work experience under your belt, even if it's part time work or charity work. Try to also provide examples of responsibilities during each work role and any managerial experience too. These will all work in your favour.

Motivational questions

Q. Why do you want to join the Navy? Have you considered the RAF or the Army?

Q. What specifically attracts you to the Royal Navy?

Q. When did you first want to join and has anyone influenced you in your decision to join?

Q. Who have you talked to about a career in the Royal Navy?

Q. How many visits have you had to the Armed Forces Careers Office?

Q. Have you previously attended AIB? If you have, what have you done to improve on last time?

Q. What contact have you had with the Royal Navy? Have you visited any establishments or spoken to any serving members?

Q. Are there any disadvantages for you joining?

Q. What do your family and friends think of you joining?

Q. What branch of the Royal Navy have you applied for?

Q. Would you consider any other branches of the Navy other than the one(s) you have chosen?

Q. What research have you carried out during your preparation for joining the Royal Navy?

Q. Would you consider a Non-Commissioned role if you were unsuccessful at AIB?

Q. What length of commission/service would you like to work?

Q. What qualities are required in order to become a Royal Naval Officer?

Tips – Defend your branch choice as much as possible. In order to be capable of achieving this, you will need to know it inside out. Make sure you research key information about your chosen branch/career.

Knowledge of the Royal Navy

Q. Tell me what you know about the history of the Royal Navy?

Q. What training will you undergo as an Officer?

Q. Do you think you will have any problems or face any challenges during Initial Officer Training?

Q. Have you learnt anything about other branches of the Royal Navy? For example, if you are applying to join the Fleet Air Arm, what do you know about the Engineering section?

Q. Tell me what you know about the different aircrafts that serve in the Royal Navy?

Q. Tell me what you know about the different ships that serve in the Royal Navy?

Q. Tell me what you know about the different types of weapons that are carried both on ships and on our aircraft?

Q. How would you feel about going to war?

Q. Where are the UK bases of the Royal Navy?

Q. Whereabouts in the world are the Royal Navy operating right now?

Current affairs questions

Current affairs are a very important area of your preparation. You must carry out plenty of research in relation to current affairs. Not only will you need it during the interview(s), but it will also assist you during the essay element of the AIB.

Here are a few important tips to help you research current affairs effectively:

TIP 1: Be careful what paper(s) you read. The type of paper you read will reflect you as a person. If you tell the interviewer that you are an avid reader of the Sun or the Daily Star, you may not be officer material. In the build up to AIB, try reading the Times, or another quality newspaper.

TIP 2: I would strongly recommend that you subscribe to 'The Week'. This is a fantastic journal that will break down the week's stories for you. This will save having to buy lots of different newspapers.

You can subscribe to the week at the following website:

www.theweek.co.uk

TIP 3: Consider reading the Economist. Once again, this is a quality journal that will provide you with lots of current affairs information.

You can subscribe to the Economist at the following website:
www.economist.com

TIP 4: Don't just research affairs that are relevant to the Royal Navy or the Armed Forces in general. Other topics are just as important!

The purpose of the current affairs section of the AIB interview is designed to assess how informed you are of current global affairs. You should have a general view on each subject and have an understanding of why the issue is important. Try to have a general view of the whole world with knowledge of a number of issues and events.

Use this format to help you research news and current affairs events:

- What is the subject?
- Why is it significant?
- What is your opinion on it?

Sample current affairs questions

Q. Take me on a tour of the world and tell me what's caught your eye in the news recently.

Q. Tell me about 6 current affairs from abroad and six from home.

Q. Tell me about a news story from each continent.

USEFUL WEBSITES

BBC News: www.bbc.co.uk/news/

The Times Online: www.timesonline.co.uk

NATO (North Atlantic Treaty Organisation: www.nato.int

Ministry of Defence: www.mod.uk

Army: www.army.mod.uk

Royal Navy: www.royalnavy.mod.uk

Royal Air Force: www.raf.mod.uk

FINAL INTERVIEW TIPS

- Research key affairs from across the world.
- Have a broad knowledge of current affairs.
- Research affairs that have happened in the last 12 months.
- Focus in detail on events in the last 6 month.
- Select 6 topics for 'home' affairs (e.g. the budget, gang culture).
- Select 6 topics for 'away' affairs. Make sure that you use examples from right across the world.
- Gauge an opinion of each affair (you will need to be able to argue your point).
- Know key facts: people, numbers, locations etc.
- A firm handshake demonstrates a lot about yourcharacter.
- Be to the point and concise (don't waffle).
- Hold even eye contact with each boarding officer.
- Avoid hesitations such as "erm, ah, umm etc".
- Don't use slang.
- Sit up straight and don't slouch.
- Be confident but not overly so!
- Learn the dates and events listed on your application form.
- Make yourself stand out - do something different.
- Be aware of your weaknesses.
- Identify your strengths.
- Think before you speak.

A FEW FINAL WORDS

You have now reached the end of the guide and no doubt you will be ready to start preparing for the Royal Navy Officer selection process. Just before you go off and start on your preparation, consider the following.

The majority of candidates who pass the selection process have a number of common factors. These are as follows:

1. They believe in themselves.

The first factor is self-belief. Regardless of what anyone tells you, you can pass the AIB and you can achieve high scores. Just like any job of this nature, you have to be prepared to work hard in order to be successful. The biggest piece of advice I can give you is to concentrate on matching the assessable qualities that form part of the scoring criteria. These would be at the forefront of my mind if I was going through selection right now. Make sure you have the self-belief to pass the selection process and fill your mind with positive thoughts.

2. They prepare fully.

The second factor is preparation. Those people who achieve in life prepare fully for every eventuality and that is what you must do when you apply to become an Officer with the Royal Navy. Work very hard and especially concentrate on your weak areas. Within this guide I have spoken a lot about preparation. Identify the areas that you are weak on and go all out to improve them.

3. They persevere.

Perseverance is a fantastic word. Everybody comes across obstacles or setbacks in their life, but it is what you do about those setbacks that is important. If you fail at something, then ask yourself 'why' have I failed? This will allow you to improve for next time and if you keep improving and trying, success will eventually follow. Apply this same method of thinking when you apply to join the Navy as an Officer.

4. They are self-motivated.

How much do you want to join the Royal Navy? Do you want it, or do you really want it? When you apply to join you should want it more than anything in the world. Your levels of self motivation will shine through when you walk into the AFCO and when you attend the Admiralty Interview Board. For the weeks and months leading up to the selection process, be motivated as best you can and always keep your fitness levels up as this will serve to increase your levels of motivation.

Work hard, stay focused and be what you want...

Richard McMunn

Richard McMunn

P.S. Come and spend a day with my team on the one day intensive Royal Navy Officer AIB preparation course at the following website:

NavyOfficerCourse.co.uk

how2become